Praise for *The Great*

"*The Great Wheel* offers a framework for understi̇̇̇ ing your place in the world, and choosing your ̇̇̇̇ ̇̇̇̇ ̇̇ ̇̇ oɪɪers theories and predictions and grounds them in telling the stories of characters who live the examples that are given. Additionally, there are suggestions on how to ritualize a fresh understanding of living in the seasons of history. It is a good time to read this book."

—Ivo Dominguez, author of *The Keys to Perception*

"A wonderful combination of science and soul. Graham uses deftly crafted analogues to explain academic concepts. As the analogues begin to cross into each other's stories, the variety of connections expands to include the reader, allowing them to draw parallels to themselves and to older and younger people in their lives. It's a moving way to build bridges across the generation gap, and Graham does it with casual elegance. What I found was a wonderfully researched examination of politics, intergenerational relations, and faith."

—E.K. Johnston, *New York Times* bestselling author

"In *The Great Wheel*, Graham takes Strauss and Howe's generational theory and elaborates on it from an entirely Pagan perspective, offering readers exercises and rituals to determine their own place on the wheel and to shape their choices wisely and with care. By turns down-to-earth and inspiring, practical and profound, *The Great Wheel* offers an entirely new way to think about the cycles of history and a truly Pagan way to prepare for the times to come."

—Melissa Scott, Lambda Literary Award–winning author

The
GREAT
WHEEL

© Amy Griswold

About the Author

Jo Graham is the author of twenty-five books and two online games. Best known for her historical fantasy and her tie-in novels for MGM's popular *Stargate Atlantis* and *Stargate SG-1* series, she has been a Locus Award finalist, an Amazon Top Choice, a Spectrum Award finalist, a Romantic Times Top Pick in historical fiction, and a Lambda Literary Award and Rainbow Award nominee for bisexual fiction. With Melissa Scott, she is the author of five books in the Order of the Air series, a historical fantasy series set in the 1920s and '30s within a Hermetic lodge.

She has practiced in Pagan and Hermetic traditions for more than thirty years, including leading an eclectic circle for nearly a decade. Dedicated in 1989, she took her mastery in 2004. She has studied the classical world extensively and today mainly works in traditions based on the Hellenistic Cult of Isis. Though she worked in politics for fifteen years, today Jo Graham divides her time between writing and working as a guardian ad litem for children in foster care. She lives in North Carolina with her partner and their daughters.

····· JO GRAHAM ·····

The GREAT WHEEL

LIVING THE PAGAN CYCLES OF OUR LIVES & TIMES

Llewellyn Publications
Woodbury, Minnesota

The Great Wheel: Living the Pagan Cycles of Our Lives & Times © 2020 by Jo Graham. All rights reserved. No part of this book may be used or reproduced in any manner whatsoever, including internet usage, without written permission from Llewellyn Publications, except in the case of brief quotations embodied in critical articles and reviews.

FIRST EDITION
First Printing, 2020

Cover design by Shannon McKuhen
Editing by Brian R. Erdrich
Interior art by the Llewellyn Art Department

Llewellyn Publications is a registered trademark of Llewellyn Worldwide Ltd.

Library of Congress Cataloging-in-Publication Data (Pending)
ISBN: 978-0-7387-6311-8

Llewellyn Worldwide Ltd. does not participate in, endorse, or have any authority or responsibility concerning private business transactions between our authors and the public.

All mail addressed to the author is forwarded but the publisher cannot, unless specifically instructed by the author, give out an address or phone number.

Any internet references contained in this work are current at publication time, but the publisher cannot guarantee that a specific location will continue to be maintained. Please refer to the publisher's website for links to authors' websites and other sources.

Llewellyn Publications
A Division of Llewellyn Worldwide Ltd.
2143 Wooddale Drive
Woodbury, MN 55125-2989
www.llewellyn.com
Printed in the United States of America

Forthcoming Books by Jo Graham

Winter

for my daughter Ashlee
the wheel turns

Contents

Chapter 1: The Great Year ... 1

Chapter 2: The Wheel of Life ... 11

Chapter 3: Dancing the Octaves ... 31

Chapter 4: Wheel of Time ... 43

Chapter 5: Spring-Born: 1943–1960 ... 57

Chapter 6: Summer-Born: 1961–1980 ... 69

Chapter 7: Autumn-Born: 1905–1924, 1981–2001 ... 83

Chapter 8: Winter-Born: 1925–1942, 2002–? ... 101

Chapter 9: Winter, a Season of Crisis ... 119

Chapter 10: Before the Storm ... 139

Chapter 11: Imbolc, a Time for Heroes ... 149

Chapter 12: A New Beginning ... 169

Chapter 13: The Wheel Turns, Spring-Born: (2025?–2045?) ... 197

Bibliography ... 207

Chapter 1

The Great Year

Three Thousand Years Ago

On a clear, cool morning in early spring, a group of people gathered on a hillside in central Italy. The distant mountains looked purple in the dawn, and, below, the slopes fell away to a little river. There were fields on the slopes awaiting the plow, and at the crest of the hill, a huddle of small, round wooden houses appeared hastily built, as though to get shelter as quickly as possible. The only sturdy, permanent feature was a heavy stone altar before which the people gathered.

There were only fifty or so of them, mostly young families, though the white-robed priest who stood by the kindled flame was older, a few threads of gray in his beard. A boy held the rope about the neck of a young steer, his horns garlanded with evergreen vine. The steer was the sacrifice, and he waited patiently while the people assembled. The priest looked to the sky, waiting for the moment when the rising sun topped the distant mountain peaks. A swift swallow crossed the sky, followed by its fellows, becoming a flock that dipped and soared in the first rays of the sun. A good omen, a fine omen, and he spoke aloud. "One is joined by many. So may our town grow!"

A group of girls began the hymn, praising the lord and lady of the underworld, Father Aita and Proserpina, who bring back light from darkness. The steer was led forward, the sickle knife flashed, and his blood poured out over the new-built altar. His entrails were read, good omens duly noted, while the meat was carved up by the cooks to roast over a hot fire, beef for everyone on this festal day.

On his mother's shoulder, a little boy not yet a year old watched the proceedings wide-eyed, raising his hands and shouting with excitement. The priest spoke to his parents, then touched his forehead gently with blood-stained fingers. "Remember," he said quietly. "Remember. Today this town was born."

Eighty-Three Years Later

It was a damp morning at the end of winter, and the last snow made a scant crust on the paving stones of the street. The young priest made his way carefully through the melting slush and knocked on the door of the sturdy house snug beneath its ornamented tile roof. The door opened.

A woman near her seventh decade opened it, her gray hair pinned up in neat rolls that began over her ears and ended at the nape of her neck. Her eyes were red from crying.

"Is he gone then?" the priest asked.

She nodded. "He drew his last breath just before dawn. Thank you for coming."

The priest followed her in past the shrine beside the door to the bedroom at the back of the house. A young man stood as he entered the small room; two other women gathered around the bed. There were no windows, only the light of a clay lamp hanging on chains from the ceiling, and it cast moving shadows across the face of the old man. He lay in repose, his hands crossed on his breast, his face peaceful in death.

The priest spoke to each person what words of comfort he had, and there were many—a good life well lived, a long life, a peaceful death in his own home with his daughter and his grandsons and his granddaughters-in-law, with five great-grandchildren sleeping in the house—a respected man, a man who had done much and given much, who would now lie in his family tomb. There were words of farewell, but they were as much sweet as bitter.

When all had been said, the priest saw himself out and walked the short distance to the temple. There, before the altar of Father Tinia, his acolytes waited to put out the fires. This was no ordinary death. Through the day, in ones and twos, people came and went from the temple to see the ashes, the flameless hearth. They had never seen it before. They would never see it again, save perhaps some child now carried in a mother's arms.

The temple was dark that night. The old man went to his tomb, and in the morning, light was kindled. Everyone was there, everyone who could fit in the broad square outside.

The priest raised his arms for silence. For a long moment, only the cold wind off the distant mountains spoke. "The last person who was here when our town was founded has died, and with him has passed the great year, the saeculum. No one now lives who was here before it, and so with this begins our second saeculum, our second year as a town." His eyes roved over the crowd, pausing on the faces of young children. "One of these little ones here today will see our second saeculum out, and with their passing we will begin again, our third great year. We light our fires anew." Flame was kindled, and smoke went up to the sky. Time began again.

The Saeculum

The Etruscans marked time like most ancient peoples, by the cycles of the moon and sun. Their ritual calendar survives in fragmentary form, telling us the names of their celebrations and rites, the way they danced the Wheel of the Year. An extraordinary document, the Brontoscopic Calendar, was intended as a guide for priests to help them interpret thunder omens and lists what events were predicted should thunder occur. The Brontoscopic Calendar is organized into twelve months with the year beginning in June and contains dozens of entries that provide a window into Etruscan society.[1]

However, in addition to the holidays and holy days that marked the annual Wheel of the Year, the Etruscans also measured time by the great year,

---

1. Jean Macintosh Turfa, "The Etruscan Brontoscopic Calendar and Modern Archaeological Discoveries," Etruscan Studies, Volume 10, Article 13, University of Massachusetts at Amhurst, Amhurst, MA, 2007

the saeculum. The saeculum was, quite simply, a long human lifetime. We have the misconception that before the modern era everyone died young. This is not true. While it is true that today fewer people die young, the absolute length of a human lifetime hasn't changed. In the ancient world there were people who lived into their eighties and nineties: for example, Pharaoh Ramesses II was in his nineties when he died based on examination of his mummy, while Ptolemy Soter was eighty-four according to documentary evidence. Because of high infant and child mortality and deaths from childbirth and curable diseases, fewer people lived to advanced age and the average life expectancy was lower, but the length of a long human lifetime has remained stable.

When a momentous event occurred—for example, the founding of a town—a new era was said to have dawned. This saeculum, this era, continued until everyone who had experienced the event had died. Then a new saeculum began.[2] Other momentous events were not so positive. A disaster like a volcanic eruption or a cataclysmic conflict like the Trojan War also marked the beginning and end of saecula. These life-changing events literally touched every person in a society, providing a touchstone and forever marking the lives of those who lived through them.

We are no different from the ancients in this way. World War II is an example of an enormous crisis that touched every person in the United States who was alive at the time, whether they were a soldier or the parent of a soldier, a worker on the home front, a child hastily conceived by a father they never knew, someone who migrated hundreds of miles to a new job, someone who lost all they had when they fled to America or someone who found new opportunities because of the GI Bill. Every single person who was alive at the time has a story of World War II and their part in these momentous events.

Today, those people are fewer and fewer. There will come a time in the next decade or so when everyone who actually remembers World War II is gone. Stories will remain, diaries and photographs, movies and music, mem-

---

2. Nancy Thomson de Grummond, *Etruscan Myth, Sacred History, and Legend*, University of Pennsylvania, Philadelphia, PA, 2006, 42–43

oirs and clothes and artifacts, but there will be no one who can firsthand tell you what they thought and felt and experienced. It will become history, passing out of living memory. A new saeculum will dawn in response to some new Crisis era, and we will all remember "where we were when..."

However, Crisis eras don't happen randomly. Saecular boundaries are not pliable. The Great Wheel, like the Wheel of the Year, follows a stable pattern that repeats age upon age, moving to the rhythm of human life. Exploring that pattern and understanding it is the subject of this book.

I first encountered these ideas in December 1992. I was working in Carolina Place Mall in Charlotte, North Carolina, doing mall-intercept market research—the kind where people with clipboards interrupt your shopping to ask if you will do a survey about dishwashing liquid or movies or personal hygiene products. Despite graduating from a prestigious university, I had just discovered that a liberal arts degree and three dollars would buy you a cup of coffee. We were in a recession, all of my friends were in the same circumstances, and we all felt like failures. After all, at our ages our parents had been able to buy houses! They had cruised out of college in the 1950s and 1960s to great jobs with benefits, able to buy new cars and live the American dream. What was wrong with us? Were we just slackers unable to do better than retail or pizza delivery? What was with the interviews where four hundred people applied for the same job and you knew the one who was going to get it was the owner's nephew? Were we all just losers?

On my dinner break one evening as I looked through the food court newsstand, my eye fell on a magazine cover—a bewhiskered, serious older man on a bicycle glaring at a young man on a dirt bike with a pizza balanced on the handlebars, the headline reading something like "The New Generation Gap?" I picked it up, though I didn't usually read *The Atlantic*. I dipped into the article, which was written by sociologists William Strauss and Neil Howe.[3]

I was fascinated. Here was sociological theory of the kind I had studied in college that applied directly to my experiences and those of my peers. In

---

3. William Strauss and Neil Howe, "The New Generation Gap," *The Atlantic Monthly*, December 1992

a nutshell, it explained that my generation was coming of age in completely different circumstances than the Baby Boomers or the Silent Generation before them, and that because our situation was different, our outcomes were also different. In other words, our failure to attain the economic stability our parents had at our age was not our personal failure, but a fact of life—we faced challenges that they had not, including a saturated labor market filled with young Baby Boomers who were still holding entry-level jobs because there were not enough positions for all of them to move up, a global economy that meant we were competing with cheaper labor in other markets, and an American recession instead of the American High, the postwar period of prosperity in the fifties and sixties. It was eye-opening. Furthermore, the article posited that we, as a society, had been here before. This was part of a natural cycle, and my generation stood where the Lost Generation had stood before us.

A few weeks later, over the holidays, I shared the article with my late cohort Greatest Generation father, who had graduated from college on the GI Bill in 1951. He too was fascinated. He nodded thoughtfully. "Now I see why I often think you're more like my parents than like me," he said. "My dad had to hustle. There was no safety net. There was no job security in the Great Depression. You took a gamble and if you were smart and lucky, you won. And if you didn't, you crashed. Here we are again."

I bought the book by the same authors that came out a few months later, *13th Gen: Abort, Ignore, Retry, Fail?*, and once again shared it with my father. This book delved deeper than an article could, talking about their cyclical theory of American history in greater detail, and once again what my father and I kept coming back to was this: here we are again. We are not lost in the wilderness without a map. The map is right here—the history of what has happened, the repeating patterns that nature is made up of. My father was a scientist. He looked for patterns. Things don't happen just once but follow cycles even if those cycles are the long cycles of geologic time that he studied, the centuries or thousands of years between major floods or volcanic events. Even if the cycle is too long for a human to experience, it is still there—ice ages come and the ice creeps south, warming happens and the glaciers retreat. These cycles were intuitive, the rhythms of human life, the patterns clearly evident in the lives of people we knew. We could trace their paths like the lines on our hands, similar but shaped by differing experiences.

In the years after my father's death, as I studied in various Neopagan traditions and led an eclectic magical working group for more than a decade, I became more aware of how the pattern Strauss and Howe described was exactly the same pattern as the Wheel of the Year writ large—their wheel included the Crisis era (Winter) leading to the High era (Spring), the Awakening era (Summer), the Unraveling era (Autumn), and then back to Crisis.[4] I read more of their work and could clearly see how the patterns they described were not only historically applicable but explained the contemporary political and social environment. We live in a series of nesting circles—the twenty-four-hour wheel of day and night, the annual Wheel of the Year, the human lifetime Great Wheel of the saeculum, and the long cycles of geologic time. These insights brought me more than a sense of personal and spiritual understanding. They provided a road map to the future. If, as Shakespeare says, "there is a tide in the affairs of men which taken at flood leads on to fortune," knowing when and what that tide might be could be invaluable. If I knew that my generation could not win using the tried and true techniques we were taught by parents and teachers who grew up in a different time, if I knew we could not win with professionally printed resumes or playing it safe, if I knew that my actions had to move in concert with the season rather than against the movement of the wheel, I had an enormous advantage.

Ten years after I worked in the mall, I went to Washington, DC, as the southern field director for the Human Rights Campaign, having previously worked on winning congressional and senate races and having been the executive director of Equality NC. Being out and queer was supposed to be the kiss of death in terms of a career. I made it a tremendous advantage. Having a child was supposed to be impossible in a time when being out in a state

---

4. William Strauss and Neil Howe, *Generations: The History of America's Future*, Morrow and Company, New York, NY, 1991

where same-sex sexual activity was still a felony and queer parents regularly lost their children to CPS. My partner and I did it. Our toddler child went before the national press corps with us in 2004, the face of a child who would be harmed by the Federal Marriage Amendment.

In 2005 I gave a presentation to a group of national LGBT activists on generational theory and why we were going to win on LGBT rights issues if we could simply prevent negative legislation until 2020. Analyzing polling data across various platforms, including Gallup and Pew, I showed that the rise of the Millennial voter would ensure that anti-gay legislation was doomed after 2020, and that while it might have seemed in 2005 that we faced a backlash and a cultural turn against us, we were actually winning; our strategy had to be to prevent a constitutional amendment not easily undone. This informed the national strategy of the LGBT rights movement in the early 2000s.

Of course, the other side of the political arena has also taken note of Strauss and Howe's work, making its own predictions.[5] However, these generational theories do not belong to any one political group any more than the Wheel of the Year belongs to any one Pagan tradition. The cycles simply are. The tides are apolitical and areligious. What ships catch the tide is up to the sailors. Just as heathenry, Asatru, and in fact all Neopagan movements are too important to simply surrender to bad actors who wish to misuse them to oppress others, the Great Wheel is also too important to surrender. We need to embrace and understand these cyclical concepts as Pagans and as members of society, both for the improvement of our own lives, and in order to change the world for the better. We are part of history. We dance the pattern of the Great Wheel every day, every year, and throughout our lives.

We are responsible keepers of our world and our society, called to take part in the challenges of our age. To do that, we need to understand better how the cycles that govern it work. My father studied the natural cycles of floods in part to help communities prepare for and prevent natural disasters, and to help individuals survive when catastrophes occurred. This book closely examines the historical cycles put forth by Strauss and Howe through

---

5. Jeremy W. Peters, "Bannon's Views Can Be Traced to a Book That Warns, 'Winter Is Coming,'" *The New York Times*, April 8, 2017

a Pagan worldview that already embraces the concept of living on an ever-turning wheel. Drawing on our deep spiritual connection to the annual turning of the seasons, we can better prepare for and prevent human tragedies and navigate the challenges of each season through this deeper examination and understanding of the great year. I welcome you to walk this path with me.

First, we will explore our personal wheels of life, the seasons of a human life, through exercises, journaling, and meditations. Then through stories we will explore the great year in the United States in the twentieth and twenty-first centuries, and how we relate to this movement of time. Lastly, we will come to understand the saecular season of Winter, what Strauss and Howe refer to as a "Crisis era," in which we currently find ourselves. With stories, rituals, meditations, and exercises, we will fortify ourselves for Winter and walk through the turning season into Spring. Together, we will walk the Great Wheel.

Chapter 2

The Wheel of Life

All of us, as we grew up, internalized one of three understandings about how time works. This is because there are three main visions in our culture today and we are all products of our culture. Time is linear, chaotic, or cyclical.

Linear time is the most common view in Western culture. In this view of history, things happen in a rational order based on cause and effect, and everything is an upward trend line. Since the Renaissance, everything has been continually improving; science, industry, business, and social science are all about growing, becoming more "advanced," rational, and fair. Progress is the keyword. Everything is supposed to become bigger and better all the time, and downward turns are the result of uncomfortable and unnecessary interruptions in that progress. We are continually moving away from darkness and toward light.

This view, though expressed differently, is also the basis of conservative Christian thought. The story of Creation is linear from Adam to Moses to Jesus to the book of Revelation. The End Times are the last chapter in the story, which has a beginning, middle, and end as a linear narrative—the story of the world. The apocalypse, whether it happens in ten years or ten thousand, is the ultimate end. We are moving through the chapters between, and things happen in accordance with God's will rather than as part of natural cycles.

The chaotic view of history is best expressed as "stuff happens." People do some things, and some things happen. Or sometimes things just happen—people are minding their own business and somebody drops a bomb on them or a plague occurs or a volcano erupts and a tsunami destroys everything they know. There's no logic or purpose to it. There's no real pattern. Sometimes people go nuts and kill each other and sometimes they don't. There's no point in trying "to read the tea leaves" about what the future holds because it's essentially chaotic and unknowable.

The third view is that history is cyclical, and according to the scholars William Strauss and Neil Howe, this is the oldest human vision of time.[6] Ancient peoples observed the cycles of the natural world—the tides, the phases of the moon, and the Wheel of the Year—and drew the conclusion that everything was part of a recurring cycle. Some cycles, like the tides, were very short and could be observed going through a full cycle daily. Others required many days, like the phases of the moon. Still others required many moons to make a full circle of the seasons. Others required even longer, many years to make up the cycle of a human life span. While individual events varied from cycle to cycle, a pattern could be detected that allowed people to plan and prepare. A ship can be launched on the high tide, crops can be planted at the beginning of the growing season, and children can be taught in expectation that they will mature into adults; they will not remain perpetually children, nor will they regress back into childhood as adults.

Most modern Pagan traditions embrace a cyclical view of time as most ancient Pagan religions did. Strauss and Howe went through great pains to explain how cyclical time works as a basis for understanding history because most modern Americans do not understand the concept. Neopagans are at an extraordinary advantage here. We are familiar with the Wheel of the Year even if our own practices do not emphasize it, and we certainly have an understanding of time as marked by various natural cycles, rather than as linear and unrepeating or without any rhythm or pattern at all.

---

6. William Strauss and Neil Howe, *The Fourth Turning*, Broadway Books, New York, NY, 1997

In this book we will use the model of the Celtic Wheel of the Year and its eight quarters and cross quarters as a tool for understanding the larger wheels of cyclical time. There are two reasons for this: firstly, because this is a model familiar to most modern Pagans, whether their tradition uses it or not, and secondly because of the geography of the United States. While the Etruscans and early Romans lived in a Mediterranean climate with three seasons, most of the United States, with the exception of Southern California, is not in such a climate zone. Jennifer Reif describes this Mediterranean cycle in her Demetrian Wheel of the Year—planting in the wet season, which begins in October, harvest in April, May, and June, and the fallow period of drought from Midsummer to after Autumn Equinox.[7] However, to follow that pattern for this book would not be intuitive for the majority of readers who experience a four-season wheel, or are familiar with it even if they live in tropical Florida or boreal Alaska.

So too, later Roman religion was modified as it traveled to areas outside a Mediterranean climate, meshing with the beliefs of peoples who lived in other geographical areas, creating hybrid beliefs that are with us today. This book does not seek to recreate ancient beliefs, but rather find relevance for those beliefs in the modern world and draw insights from them for our lives in the twenty-first century United States.

The Wheel of the Year

First, let's briefly review the Wheel of the Year as it is typically understood today. Again, different traditions use different terminology, so please substitute whatever terminology is most comfortable to you. The purpose is to create a model useful for you, not to authoritatively state a single terminology. Different traditions begin the year at different points on the wheel, but the wheel goes round, and no matter what your starting point, it is the same dance. In this book we will begin at the Spring Equinox.

The Spring Equinox, at the far right-hand side of the wheel, is the beginning of astronomical spring. In the Northern Hemisphere this is between

---

7. Jennifer Reif, *The Mysteries of Demeter,* Samuel Weiser and Associates, York Beach, ME, 1999, 73–78

March 19 and 22, depending on the year, when we are halfway through the cycle from the shortest day of the year to the longest day of the year. In some parts of the United States, snow may still be on the ground, while in others, spring flowers may be blooming and trees already growing new leaves. Either way, the Spring Equinox is a time of beginning, of completing the return from the darkness of Midwinter, of new growth and new opportunity.

From the Spring Equinox, we progress clockwise around the wheel to Beltane on May 1. One of the great fire festivals, Beltane is a celebration of heady, full-blown spring, often marked with competitions and dancing, with nights in the greenwood and the choosing of a May Queen. Beltane celebrates sexuality and athletics and even danger, with traditional competitions like fire-leaping that can go badly for the participants. Beltane is for joy and taking chances.

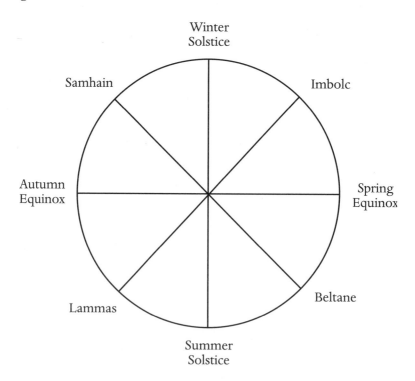

Moving clockwise, we reach the Summer Solstice, or Midsummer, the point on the wheel that occurs between June 19 and 22 in the Northern Hemisphere.

Midsummer is the longest day of the year, when the sun seems to remain in the sky until very late. It is the time of growing things, of abundant daylight and warmth, of all things striving for maximum growth while conditions are ideal. Traditionally, this is a time for marriages and handfastings.

Continuing around the wheel, the next point is Lammas, on August 1. This is the first harvest, and in many parts of the United States, this is when corn ripens and other fresh vegetables and fruits are plentiful. It is a celebration of these harvests and of the brightness of summer days, the "dog days," the heat of the year when thoughts turn to beaches and lakeshores. The days are not as long, reminding everyone that summer will come to its end and, in a few short weeks, school buses will ply the streets.

Next is the Autumn Equinox, halfway between Midsummer and Midwinter, falling in the Northern Hemisphere between September 19 and 22. This is the second harvest. In some parts of the country it still feels like summer, while in other parts there is a distinct chill in the air, but either way, the natural world is moving appreciably toward winter. Crops are finishing, pumpkins ripening, and perhaps the leaves are already changing color.

Continuing clockwise, we reach Samhain on October 31, the date conventionally known as Halloween. This is the last harvest, when final preparations for winter are made and the last crops come in. This is also the ancient day of the dead, a time for celebrating ancestors and those who have gone before. Today, it is also the festival of misrule, when people dress up in costumes and try on other, more forbidden, identities.

The next point on the circle is Midwinter, the Winter Solstice, which occurs around December 21. This is when the nights are longest and the days are shortest. Though often the worst of winter weather is yet to come, by Midwinter it is truly winter and nature has reached a fallow period. For some winter may be harsh and for others milder, but winter is a time of gathering in and celebrating ties of family and warmth.

Lastly, we come all the way around the circle to Imbolc on February 1. This is the depths of winter, the coldest time of the year in many locations, though the days have begun to lengthen. This is traditionally a time to celebrate craft and stories, to concentrate on things that are done indoors and improve life rather than just providing food. It is a time of introspection and turning inward as the outside world is inhospitable.

And then the wheel turns, and we return to the Spring Equinox. The cycle of the Wheel of the Year is now complete. Now we will scale up and examine a larger cycle, the Wheel of Life.

The Roman Wheel of Life

The Romans, the physical and spiritual heirs of the Etruscans, divided human life into stages. While there were several different means of making the divisions, the most influential was described by the poet Horace and was composed of four stages corresponding to the natural seasons of the earth, each stage being approximately twenty years long.

Pueritia (childhood) corresponds with spring, a time of growth and new beginnings, of learning and commencing new things.

Iuventus (youth) corresponds with summer, a time of competition and fertility, of heated blood and heated thoughts, of striving and reaching.

Virilitas (maturity, adulthood) corresponds with autumn, a time of harvest and building, of ruling and governing.

Senectia (old age) corresponds with winter, a time of completion and wisdom, of decline and letting go, of turning inward.[8]

Each person, unless they die young and untimely, experiences each of these stages of life once. The Wheel of the Year echoes our Wheel of Life. We are born with the spring, mature into summer, gather and rule with autumn, and at last step back as the keepers of wisdom with winter. Whatever our personal path, we have no choice but to proceed through the wheel in seasonal order. Each person may have unique gifts and experiences at each stage, but it is not possible to simply stay in one season or to reverse or change direction. Nobody proceeds from childhood to maturity without passing through youth, and nobody can go from maturity to youth rather than the other way around.

---

8. Christian Laes and Johan Strubbe, *Youth in the Roman Empire*, Cambridge University Press, Cambridge, UK, 2014, 24–26

The Octaves

A more detailed view of the Wheel of Life might be to begin with the classical Greco-Roman quadrants and divide them once again by adding the cross quarters of the Wheel of the Year, thereby creating a circle with eight sections, the octaves. The advantage of this is that it more closely shows the changes that occur within a quadrant. For example, a child two years old and a teen eighteen years old are not learning the same things, developing the same skills or having anything like the same experiences, even if, according to the classical model, they are both in the quadrant of pueritia. They are both in spring, absolutely, but the two-year-old is at the very beginning, barely past the Spring Equinox, while the high school senior is well into the heady season after Beltane and rapidly approaching summer.

Therefore, let's consider a wheel divided into octaves, each approximately thirteen years long, a traditional magical number. Of course each individual does not necessarily experience changes exactly on the numbered birthday or during that year, but these represent general parameters. For example, the age of thirteen is a traditional time for coming of age ceremonies for adolescents, marking the boundary at the end of childhood. However, that varies. While boys may bar mitzvah at thirteen, it's not unusual to be fourteen. Not every girl will have her first menses at thirteen—some are older and some younger. Not every rite and traditional ceremony happens exactly at thirteen—a quinceañera is at fifteen. First Communion may be at eleven or twelve. An individual's experiences may vary.

With that in mind, let's consider the octaves of the Wheel of Life.

Spring Equinox to Beltane: Beginning

Dawn on the first morning of spring. The air is cool and crisp. The branches of the trees are still bare. And yet the air is full of birdsong. Sunrise brings a chorus, every bird takes flight, seeking food and a mate. Through the loam of last autumn's leaves poke the green stems of daffodils, bursting into blooms of white and yellow, cups turning toward the nascent sun, flowering in great drifts under the trees while pear and cherry trees shower petals of pink and white. The world is born again, revitalized. On a morning like this, anything could happen. All is bright potential.

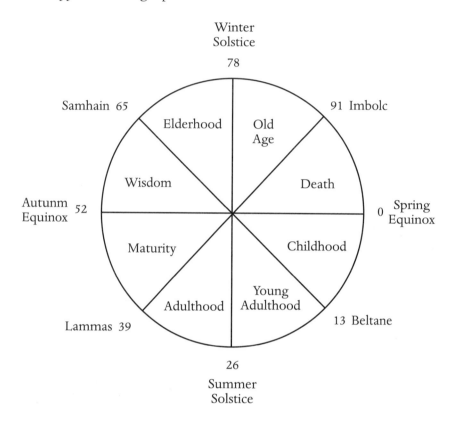

We are born with the spring. On this day, the Spring Equinox, a baby opens her eyes for the first time. They are yet unfocused, unable to see more than twelve inches from her face, but she stares intently at everything close enough, reaching upward toward a face, a hand, a bright toy. In this moment, she could do anything. She could be an Olympian, a scientist, a priestess, a scholar. All the potentials are there, all the beginnings possible. Every dream is alive, every wonderful future imagined. She begins with the spring.

But just as every first green shoot does not turn into a great tree, so every child does not reach every pinnacle. Some shoots are not trees. Some are eggplant or corn to feed the hungry. Some are briefly blooming summer flowers. Some are sturdy holly bushes that provide shelter and food for birds.

Some are butterfly weed and some roses. And some are never anything. A spring frost cuts them to the bone, leaving shriveled and frozen shoots on the ground. Some are washed away by too much rain. Some die for lack of water. Not every child thrives. Spring is beautiful and full of potential, but it has its hazards as well. Small lives are vulnerable.

Assuming we pass through these spring storms, aided by those with watering cans and timely row covers, the days wax warmer. The sprouting seed gets its second leaves and then its third. We begin to see what sort of plant it is.

So too do first talents and interests begin to emerge—the child who loves cars and anything that has a motor, the one who loves dinosaurs and memorizes endless facts about them, the one who plays teacher and lines stuffed animals up to learn and be cuddled. Is this a mechanic or race car driver or engineer? A scientist? A teacher? We try to guess. We imagine futures just as the child does, trying on capes and costumes. Am I a superhero? A ballerina? An artist? A firefighter? What is their land of imagination? "What do you want to be when you grow up?"

Halfway between the Spring Equinox and Beltane is six and a half years, half of the thirteen years of the octave. By this point most children are in school, and play is beginning to gain a more serious tone. They are expected to read and write, to learn math and science, to sit still in a classroom for periods of time. So too does informal play turn into lessons for many children—throwing a softball around the yard becomes peewee league softball, dressing in tutus becomes dance lessons, tooting on a kazoo becomes after-school music lessons.

Of course not all children have this. Lack of opportunity means that many do not explore their interests and do not have the chance to develop talents. Some growing shoots receive ample water and sun. Others do not. Some attend terrible schools. Some live in unsafe circumstances without adequate food or shelter. Some are abused by those they trust. Some are denied opportunities because of social inequalities. And some persevere despite all disadvantages, growing straight and strong, putting forth green leaves even in the most dreadful situations.

Growth wins. In spring, the drive to reach for the sun is inexorable. More! More ideas, more energy, more interests, more freedom—more! Bigger than last year, better than last time, stronger and taller, brighter and finer—more! Seven to twelve is a time of reaching. The days lengthen. Tomorrow will be longer and brighter than today.

Beltane to Midsummer: Becoming

Adolescence crashes in like the sound of trumpets. Thirteen years old, or thereabouts, and the child has become a teenager. It's a magical word. Not twelve, but thirteen. Not a preteen, but a teen. Beltane has come.

These are the first really warm days when you can feel the heat of the sun growing. The daffodils and snowdrops are gone, replaced by azaleas and mountain laurels spilling fuchsia blooms in great drifts. Fragile pinks and yellows give way to brighter hues, games to competitions, to a heat in the blood.

When did he get so tall? Where did those long legs come from? And that voice—did it just break? She has a figure, curves that weren't there before. She's not a cute child—she's beautiful. Bodies change, taking on their adult forms. Hair grows, menses begin, breasts grow, and suddenly there are all these angles and tones that weren't there before. Adolescence is a period of profound physical change. Children stop being children. They become young adults.

This is hard and painful. The years from thirteen to twenty are full of new opportunities filled with hazards and hopes. Interests turn to passions, talents into budding proficiency. There's a moment when you listen to the wild guitar playing, look at the newly drawn graphic novel, stand up cheering for the slam dunk, when you say, "Wow, you're really *good!*" Actually good, not just potentially good—an adult peering out on the first blossoms opening to the sun. This is the time to follow those passions; young adults get their first jobs, choosing one set of classes, one career path, over another. This is the first time those choices matter. Before Beltane, a child could be a firefighter today, a dancer tomorrow, and a doctor the day after, all in play. Now the choices are real. You can be a firefighter or a dancer or a doctor, but not all of them. Not all at once. The decision to pursue a career in the arts means not going into a pre-med program and vice versa. You can't do a community college program in firefighting while dancing professionally. One or the other. The stakes are high: the choices are real and often final.

Summer has its rewards. Long days, everything getting hotter and hotter, warm sun and warm skin, loud music and open roads, sweltering nights and bonfires, wild, whirling dances—summer is a feast for the senses, a heat in the blood and the heart. Sexuality, a mystery uncovered at Beltane, beckons the initiate. Who do you want? Who are you to want? Where will the tides of life draw you? Will they pull to happiness or sorrow? Will these overwhelming, bursting waves carry you far out to sea or pull you under?

Summer is competition. Are you the best? Are you the strongest athlete, the smartest writer, the boldest musician, the bravest soldier? Will you draw blood on the field or with the pen? Will you bleed yourself in a squeal of brakes and a crashing, crumpling of metal and flesh against the concrete barrier in the middle of the highway? Or will it be more—not a self-imposed test of nerves and courage and carelessness, but will it be war? Will it be an IED or bomb, or even the falling timbers of a burning building that bear the rookie firefighter down beneath them?

Blood. Sex. Fire. By the time half the octave has passed, by the age of twenty, the dangers are real and so are the rewards.

Somewhere between seventeen and twenty-one another milestone is passed for most American teens: moving out and living on their own. Whether to a college dorm, a military barracks, or an apartment with friends or partners, most people make their first try at living on their own at about this time. For many, this is the passage to adulthood, a process begun at Beltane with adolescence, now completed with their physical autonomy. And yet for most this is not full integration into adult society, "adulting," as it is sometimes called. "Adulting" is what takes up the rest of the octave, the years from twenty or so to twenty-six or so, to life's Midsummer.

Simply put, this is the time for making a life that works. Does the person have the skills they need to support themselves? Can they do work that has meaning both financially and personally? Can they form relationships with friends, lovers, mentors, bosses, and family that are happy and positive? Can they begin to give back as an equal partner, a productive employee, or as a parent themselves? Can they create things that are meaningful and contribute to society? At this point, these are beginnings. Very few people have achieved their life's work by the time they're twenty-six! Unless they're an athlete or an artist in a field that peaks young, most people have little to show by their mid-twenties—they have begun, but not yet achieved. And that is as it should be.

In the garden, only a few vegetables are ripe at Midsummer. Peas, lettuces, maybe the earliest squash—but mostly the garden is green. There are green tomatoes, pumpkin vines running across the yard, sweet melons round and tiny, just-setting fruit. But they have begun. Lammas' fragrant tomatoes and Samhain's orange pumpkins cannot exist without Midsummer's vines. If they are not planted by Midsummer, they will never ripen.

And there is the cruelty. Infinite potential is gone. Things not begun will not be completed. There is no longer all the time in the world, even when it feels like there is. The wheel is turning. Fertility has its limits. Enlistment is only an option until a certain age. Peers are racing forward, claiming the entry level positions, making their first marks. Those who are left behind will have a hard time catching up. The boundaries may not have been reached yet, but they are approaching. There is no longer infinite time for beginning.

Midsummer to Lammas: Responsibility

Midsummer has been reached, and though most of summer lies ahead, each day the sun sets a little sooner. These hot days immediately after Midsummer are the time for second chances, for rectifying mistakes, for changing course. The degree abandoned can be completed at a different school in a different subject. The second marriage or serious relationship, the second job, the second career path, all promise to be better than the first. In one's late twenties, there is the opportunity to shift.

There is also the opportunity to add, to take on the second thing in addition to the first. Maybe school was his goal, and dating took second place to a challenging degree. Now it's done. He has it. Now he looks at his friends with their wives, husbands, or lovers and says, "Wait, did I miss something?"

Maybe it's going to a party and someone has brought their baby, a wave of something entirely new touching him as he watches his friend holding his baby daughter. "Did I need that? Do I want that? Why do I suddenly feel this stirring, this desire to nurture and protect, this dad waking up inside me?"

Or maybe what's shifted is the ability to make dreams manifest. Sure, he's always drawn cartoons, but now, thirty years old with a job doing something else, he's drawing a web series. People are following it, telling him he's good, telling him it should be compiled and published. He's disciplined about it now, drawing every day, making sure he posts new material every Tuesday and Friday. Where did this control come from? He used to struggle to get assignments in, and this isn't an assignment. It's a self-imposed deadline. Nobody will dock his paycheck or fail him if he doesn't post, but he's staying up to finish, planning ahead to cover busy days.

Responsibility is the keyword of the octave between Midsummer and Lammas. No longer a passenger in the world, now is the time to do. By halfway through the octave, in one's early thirties, real responsibility sets in. It matters what you do, not just for your future but for everyone who depends on you. She is no longer the student, no longer the trainee, but the pilot flying a Hurricane Hunter aircraft into a tropical storm. Has it become a hurricane? What is its course? Hundreds of thousands of people depend on her data to know whether to evacuate or stay. Hundreds of lives depend on her accuracy and her courage.

A good teacher changes lives, and a poor one has impacts felt through a child's life. A competent nurse saves lives, and a poor one can lose them. A savvy reporter uncovers dangerous corruption and an irresponsible one misleads the public. Real responsibility. The child has become the hero.

Or not. This is the point where failure becomes truly painful, not just for the individual but for society. Twisted to the shadow, each opportunity has a terrible side: the abusive parent, the lying reporter, the lazy social worker, the selfish artist who uses their talent to hurt feelings and widen divisions. And there are those who simply do nothing. Their gardens lie fallow. Seeds are planted, but nothing is ever tended, nothing ever grows to maturity. Life courses begin and are abandoned in perpetual adolescence, always "going to do something" but never doing it, a wasteland of uncompleted projects.

And there are those who die. Illness takes some, uncompleted trajectories. Accidents take others. Some give their lives, the young firefighter killed doing their duty, the mother who drowns getting her child out of a rip current. We laud the young heroes who die for others, and we mourn those who stepped off the wheel untimely because of accident or illness.

Lammas to Autumn Equinox: Maturity

The wheel turns. Lammas, thirty-nine years old, more or less at one's fortieth birthday, is the door into midlife. This is the completion of the Roman stage iuventus and the beginning of virilitas, maturity. The garden is nearing the first harvest. Half of life's course is run.

And how sweet the harvest is! Tomatoes, corn, squash, zucchini, eggplant, peaches, melons of all types—the bounty is fantastic. It's dizzying, so many things to do, so much work to be done. In older times, harvest was the busiest time of the year. After all, there were just a few short weeks to "put up" each wonderful thing, to preserve its freshness and value as a food for the rest of the year. Pickles, preserves, relishes, and jams—picking and peeling, boiling and pureeing, hours of chopping and hot baths and boiling down and sealing—enormous amounts of work to get the harvest in and keep it.

The octave from Lammas to Autumn Equinox, roughly from thirty-nine to fifty-two, is the season of too much. There is simply too much to do and too few hours in the day. Work, home, relationship, children, even aging parents, crowd one's life to bursting. And still there are more demands. There are bills and creditors, organizations and causes, friends and personal goals, health and spirituality. The season of the first harvest is the season of plenty, but somehow no matter how many zucchinis you pick there are still more turning into giant baseball bats under the leaves. In midlife, you carry the world.

Where once she assisted on cases, now she's the lead attorney preparing for trial. Where once she relied on her parents, now they rely on her, and Dad's having heart problems and is scheduled for tests the day the case goes to trial. Oh, and the fifteen-year-old is supposed to start driving classes before school at seven a.m. And her husband has a business trip to Montreal that week that he can't get out of. And she's supposed to go to the gym and be fit and healthy, make home cooked meals that are locally sourced, and find time for spirituality and mindfulness when every moment is completely scheduled.

In fact, every moment is scheduled at least twice! And the cat seems to be mysteriously shedding. And the car has a coolant leak. And what about the athletic shoes for the kid that you promised you'd get before soccer tryouts? Have you registered to vote? Can you volunteer to phone bank? Did you remember that you have to meet with all the junior attorneys and make sure everyone's prepared and on the same page? You're meeting and one of them isn't up to speed and the phone rings; it's the school nurse because your kid is in the office throwing up and your husband is in Montreal and sure can't pick them up. And Mom is calling to tell you that Dad's test is over but the doctor wants them to see another specialist this afternoon and that doesn't sound good at all. (Are you overweight? Did you eat too much junk food today? Should you have gone through a drive-through between the courthouse and the school? Of course not. You should have had a healthy bento box with steamed ancient grains.) And your boss is calling to say that you did fine this morning, but can you be earlier tomorrow to go over the Jones deposition?

Too much. Each thing in the garden is wonderful, but everything is ripe at once. Everything is ripe, and things neglected will rot. These summer days are long, but even the long daylight doesn't give you enough time. Is there enough time to stop and breathe the life of the garden, to pause for a moment and smell the rich, summer scent of tomatoes?

And then there are those whose gardens are bare. Storms destroyed all they had planted, or nothing was planted at all. They began again too late, and have nothing ripe yet, and wonder instead if anything will come to fruit before the cold comes. The cold is coming. It's not yet, but as this octave draws to a close, there is autumn in the air. Apples are ripening. The mornings have a slight chill. Against the high, clear sky, great flocks of geese are calling. They know what you know in your bones—summer has ended.

Autumn Equinox to Samhain: Power

The second harvest, Autumn Equinox to Samhain, is the octave of power. The years from fifty-two to sixty-five, from late midlife to retirement, are the years of authority. Whether one's mature archetype is queen or priestess, king or magician, guide or master crafter, one reaches the fullest expression of mastery. The teacher has become the principal, leading the school and overseeing all instruction. The scientist has become the team leader, guiding the research. The manager has become the executive, making the decisions that run the company or nonprofit. Chief, general, senator, executive chef, maestro, professor, director, owner and proprietor—there is no one above you, and you have become the one who is responsible for the direction of your piece of the puzzle, your part of the world.

With Midsummer came responsibility. With Lammas came achievement. With the Autumn Equinox comes power. At last it really is up to you. What will you do with it? What principles and what experiences will you base your decisions on? Will you act out of altruism or greed? Out of hope or fatalism? Out of kindness or selfishness? Will you work for justice or mercy? Will you strive for excellence in whatever you do or to reap the maximum profits before you depart the stage? Do you want money or fame, inward peace or outward service? Or do you simply strive to complete what you've begun, mastery of arts or crafts, children launched into productive and happy lives, or a spiritual quest? Whatever you choose or do not choose, it will matter. This is the season of power, and you run the world.

The octave opens in middle age, with red and golden apples hanging low on the trees. The days are warm, and the frenetic routine of the first harvest only slightly abated. But, one by one, these responsibilities begin to resolve. At fifty-two, many households include children. At sixty-five, most of those children have well and truly established independence. At fifty-two, many people still have their parents in their lives. At sixty-five, their parents have begun to pass into the night and they are the oldest living generation in their family. At fifty-two, many are still striving for penultimate positions of authority in their profession or calling. At sixty-five, most are preparing to pass those positions to others.

Now the question must be asked: what did you do? Not what are you planning to do or hoping to do, but what have you done? It may not be complete. It may be still in progress, a striving that will not end until you do, but by the end of the octave that is the question: What have you done with your power? What have you done with your purpose and passion?

Autumn closes about. Leaves turn orange and scarlet, then brown, and then are scoured from the trees by newly cold rains. Pumpkins ripen, mums make bright spots in the garden. The last apples are picked, the last winter squashes. It's time for pies and harvest gatherings, the celebration of bounty and things well done, a full larder and things brought to fruition. Ideally, the end of the octave is a time of celebration. It's time to toast in new red wine the overflowing abundance of a life well lived.

And yet for some, these celebrations never occur. Death meets them untimely, disease or accident drawing them into her embrace before they are old. For others, there is little to celebrate. Past mistakes or past mishaps destroyed all hope of a harvest. The larder is bare at Samhain, and the wind whistles around a fragile, broken shelter. Perhaps others will open their arms or their homes to those who reach this point without them, sharing mercy and love.

The day is bright but the nights grow cold. Winter comes.

Samhain to Midwinter: Wisdom

Despite cold winds, despite bare branches, for many the weeks leading to Midwinter are a time of celebration. Father Saturn shares his gifts and Serapis pours out bounty from an overflowing cornucopia. Today the old man in the red suit, Santa Claus, brings presents and joy, passing on the wealth of ages past to the new generation.

This octave is the octave of wisdom. This is the time to pass on what has been accumulated, whether this is material wealth or hard-earned wisdom, literal gold and treasures or secrets of craft and scholarship, or simply painfully gathered worldly wisdom. The years from sixty-five to seventy-eight are when one is truly an elder, often still active in the community but giving over leadership to younger people while maintaining a role as counselor. The sage is an archetype that we readily recognize—the crone in her black dress who tests the hero, the old man with the staff who guides the adventurer. It is no longer their job to go out and achieve the goal but to provide much needed guidance to those who will.

Often too it is their job to provide material support. The enchanted weapon, the secret book, and the bag of herbs are gifts from the sage. Will you send your grandchild to college? Will you teach a worthy protégé the secrets of your craft? Will you direct a young hero to the sword in the stone? Show a trickster girl how to outwit the villain? Who will wield your sword when you are gone? Who will plant your garden in the spring? How do you pass on love? This is the season for generosity. As winter winds scour and pare down, this is the time to give.

Some, of course, do not. Scrooge is the Midwinter miser who learns to become the kind patron instead, but not all Scrooges change. Some go unlamented to their graves, as the Ghost of Christmas Future shows Scrooge what his own fate might be if he does not change his ways.

In the United States today, seventy-eight is the average life expectancy.[9] Thus, the end of this octave marks the end of the average life. Half of all Americans will depart before Midwinter. It's time. As the octave closes, it's time to plan one's legacy and to think of a tomorrow in which one will not be a part. This is uniquely challenging to many, as our culture embraces the idea of eternal youth. If you just eat the right things and have the right habits you will be young forever! You will—what? Live forever? We will all die. The end of this octave asks us to recognize that fact and consider what we leave behind. What riches will we pour out for our heirs? What gifts will we bring to be remembered by?

Midwinter to Imbolc: Death

Cold winds tear the last brown leaves from the trees. Snow drifts white and silent across a landscape suddenly stilled by winter. Nothing moves. The snowlight illuminates a landscape of mounds and humps, broken by the sil-

---

9. CBS News, "Average US Life Expectancy Tops 78," June 8, 2011

houettes of trees. Birds are silent, tucked in their nests or flown away. Wildlife hunkers down to survive the cold. Even when the snow ends, under the pale white stars, the cold pierces to the bone.

By Imbolc, the child born at the Spring Equinox would be ninety-one years old. Some, a lucky few, will reach that mark, but for most of those who reached Midwinter, this is the season of death. Most will pass in their eighties. Bones stand out in old hands like tree branches against the ice. Papery skin seems as fragile as frost patterns on window panes. By Imbolc, it's time to let go.

The mourners follow your coffin to the grave, somber and serene except for the children who run ahead, playing tag among the gravestones. Friends toast you at the memorial service, raising a glass and relating once again that thing you did. Your children or protégés sing your favorite song with a catch in their throat, their hearts full of how you will be missed. What will they say about you? Who will mourn you? Who will carry on your work and tell your story? Who will carry on your bloodline? Who will be inspired by your example?

Will you hover near to hear their words? Will you speak to them in dreams? Will you send one last message of love before Death enfolds you in her arms? Winter takes you.

Imbolc to Spring Equinox: The Need to Be

The garden is empty and bare. The world lies still, wrapped in a blanket of snow. Frost limns each branch, encases each twig. Nothing moves. And yet somewhere, beneath the snow, beneath the earth, something is stirring. Roots are burrowing deep, drinking in moisture and growing. Though all is emptiness, somewhere in the dark is the need to be. You need to be.

There is you, and there is the need, a primal thing like the chick within the egg. It needs. Life needs. You need. How long it takes is impossible to know. Winter is timeless.

Roots go down. Shoots press upward toward the light, pushing through wet, cold soil. Somewhere up there is the sun, strengthening daily though the days are short, the cold intense. The sun calls. You answer. You need. You need to be. Where you have been or what you have been dreaming you don't know, but now you need something, just as the questing shoot needs the sun.

A beating heart. A body half-formed, a mind developing, bones and muscles knitting together in some secret, dark place. It needs you and you need it. There is a space, a place, a body waiting for you. Gates open. A mind awakens. You stretch limbs that are now yours again. Swimming in the dark, in the sounding waters, you move. You dream. You wake.

Spring Equinox. Somewhere, in this wide world, a baby is born. You open your eyes, take a deep breath, and the wheel begins again.

··· Chapter 3 ···

Dancing the Octaves

The octaves of the Wheel of Life are the map of our life. In this chapter we will explore how we have lived through the octaves as individuals, and how we hope to live through those that we have not yet reached. Each of us has a unique set of personal experiences, but they follow a pattern—our growth and development through the classical four stages of human life, and more specifically through the octaves. Better understanding of patterns will help us align ourselves to the Great Wheel and to see the season of life that we are presently in as part of a whole, our past, present, and future making one coherent story of which we are the main character. It is easy to get stuck in the present and to forget that we were once different than we are now, that we valued different things, had different hopes and dreams, and faced difficult challenges that we may have now overcome. It is even harder for many people to imagine that someday they will be different than they are today, and that the things they want right now are not necessarily what they will always want, or that the identities they embrace today will not be what they believe thirty years from now.

This exercise is designed to help you place your individual experiences in context of the octaves, to create your own personal Wheel of Life. Because readers are a wide variety of ages, each part of this exercise after the first one will have two sets of questions to consider, one for people who have already reached this octave and one for people for whom it is still ahead.

If you would like to, you may do this exercise over the course of a full year, matching each Sabbat with its corresponding place on the Wheel of Life. You may also do this exercise alone or with a group where each person constructs their own wheel independently and shares at the end.

You may choose to do this entire exercise in one sitting, but it may be better to do it a little at a time, concentrating on one or two octaves each time so that each set of experiences has "room to breathe" and you have time to think about each one separately. Set aside at least ten or fifteen minutes for each octave. Find a quiet place where you will not be interrupted and bring the figure below, something to write or draw with, and this book. You do not need to open sacred space for this. This is a visualization and craft, not a rite.

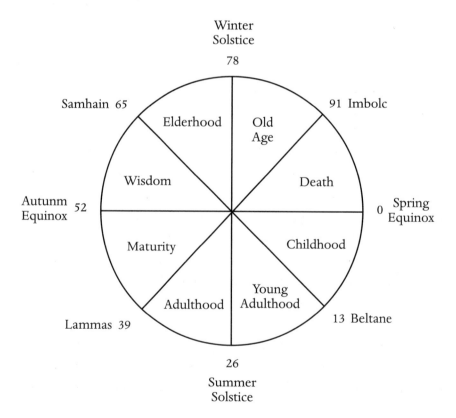

First, copy or draw the figure on the previous page, a representation of the Wheel of Life. It needs to be large enough that you have room to write in each octave. If you prefer, you can make it even bigger so that you have room to draw or to make a collage in each one instead.

The First Octave: Childhood
Birth–Age 13

Let's begin at the far right-hand side, at the point labeled Spring Equinox. The first octave is the one just clockwise of that point, between the Spring Equinox and Beltane. You may wish to reread the section on the first octave in the previous chapter. Then take a few deep breaths, center yourself, and consider the following questions:

- What is your earliest memory? Who cared for you in childhood and who did you love the most? What are the first things you remember playing? What did you want to be when you grew up? Were there any stories told about precocious talents or clever/funny things you did?

- Where did you start school? How did you feel about elementary school? Who were your best friends? What did you like to do after school? What did you dream about doing? What were your favorite stories—superheroes, movies, books, comics, or things you made up yourself?

When you've taken time to recollect, write or draw the most important things within the octave. Alternately, attach pictures or otherwise symbolize the things you remember.

This is who you were in that octave. This is where you began, where the unique story that is yours starts. Take time to think about what you've added.

The Second Octave: Youth
Ages 13–26

Let's move to the second octave, the one beginning at Beltane and moving clockwise to the Summer Solstice. Again, you may wish to reread the section on the octave in the last chapter. Take time to center yourself and consider the following questions:

- What were middle school and high school like for you? What did you excel at? What did you struggle with? Who was your first crush? What happened? Who were your best friends? How did you get along with your family? Who were the important adults in your life and how did they influence you? What did you compete to do?

- What markers were rites of passage for you? Did you have a formal ceremony or did you have more informal events? Did you learn to drive? When did you move out? Did you go to college? To other post-secondary training? Did you join the military?

- What did your first room or apartment look like—try to bring it into focus and be there. Who did you live with? What risks or gambles did you take? What goals did you pursue? Who were your mentors or role models?

- Who was your first serious relationship with? How did that unfold? What did others in your life think of it? How did that person change you?

- What hopes and fears were made manifest? How did you succeed? How did you fail? If you had it to do over, what might you do differently? What would you never change?

If you are still in this octave, some of these questions cannot yet be answered. They are yet to be. In that case, consider the following:

- What do you hope will happen? Where would you like to live and what would you like to do? Who would you like to know, either as a relationship, a friend, or a mentor? What challenges do you think you will face? What tools do you think you will need to overcome them? How can you go about getting those tools? Where do you see yourself when you are twenty-six?

These are not easy or simple questions. It may be difficult or upsetting to think about bad things that have happened or to contemplate past failures. However, our stories cannot be free from pain. Think about any hero story you know, whether an ancient or modern mythology. The hero must have setbacks. Often there are tragedies that form him or her, that provide the impetus to begin the quest. There are no stories about people nothing happens to and who do nothing. Risk and pain are essential parts of the narrative. If you are the hero of this story, it is about your trials and how you overcome them.

Let's take a modern myth many of us are familiar with—*Star Wars* hero Luke Skywalker. Luke leaves home because his aunt and uncle are brutally murdered. This is a tragedy. This is something that causes him great pain, but at the same time makes him determined to stop the Empire. Later on, when he first confronts Darth Vader, he fails. He loses spectacularly and loses his hand in the process. Only the loyalty of his friends ensures that he survives at all. But Luke learns from his failure. Instead of giving up, he takes responsibility for his mistakes and does better. The next time he confronts Darth Vader, he is better prepared and makes the choices that brings down the Empire. There are two keys here: tragedy wills you to overcome, and owning your mistakes means you can do better. That is the hero's story. The second octave is about becoming the hero.

Take time to think about what you have written or drawn.

The Third Octave: Responsibility
Ages 26–39

The third octave begins at the Summer Solstice and moves clockwise to Lammas. Again, you may wish to reread the section on the octave in the last chapter. Take time to center yourself and consider the following questions:

- What responsibilities did you take on? Family? Job? Relationships? A calling of some kind? What were the proudest moments that resulted from those responsibilities? What were the worst moments, the ones that made you squirm? What were the responsibilities that were ultimately the most rewarding?

- What kind of relationships did you have? Lovers, friends, children, partners? Did you have significant relationships with mentors or with those you mentored? What relationships disappointed you? What relationships made you happy?

- What second chances did you have? What mistakes did you rectify? What did you add to your life? How did your life follow the course you had intended and what was different? Was the change good or bad or a little of both?

- What new challenges did you face? How did you overcome them? What do you wish you'd done differently? What are you proudest of?

If you are still in this octave, or if it is ahead of you, please consider:

- What responsibilities will you undertake? Why would you choose those particular ones? What steps do you plan to take to make those outcomes manifest?

- What relationships do you hope to develop? How are you choosing to become the person who will have those relationships?

- Who do you hope to be when you are thirty-nine? What do you want to be doing in your life?

These questions aren't easy, and it may take quite some thought to come up with words to write in the octave, or to otherwise draw or illustrate. Use the space in the pie wedge of the octave to create symbols either for the path you have followed or for the hopes you wish to make manifest.

At this point, here is something to consider: We are all individuals and each of us has a different story to tell. Your story may not be like anyone else's. It will be unique. Every question may not speak to you and the events of your life, and the events that have disrupted your path may be extraordinary. That's ok. This is your story, and it is as unique as you are. The purpose of this exercise is to guide you through the generalities and milestones that are common to many people. If a particular one doesn't speak to you, simply skip it and go on.

The Fourth Octave: Accomplishment
Ages 39–52

The fourth octave begins at Lammas and moves clockwise to the Autumn Equinox. Again, you may wish to reread the section on the octave in the last chapter. Take time to center yourself and consider the following questions:

- What was in your garden? What was ripening in your life? What harvests were you already reaping?

- What demanded your time and effort? What were you striving for? What seemed overwhelming? What did you wish you could let go of? What did you wish you could devote more effort to?

- What was still growing in your garden but hadn't yet come to fruition? What were you working toward that was still ahead of you? How were you tending these plans to help them become manifest? What are your expectations for the future?

- How did the world benefit from your work? Who did you help?

If you are still in this octave, or if it is ahead of you, please consider:

- What do you want to harvest? What do you visualize reaping? Relationships? Work? Crafts or arts? Family?

- How do you measure success? What are you striving for? What rewards are most important to you? Money? Love? Connectedness? Fame or praise? Security or freedom?

- What do you want your life to look like when you are fifty-two? What do you want to have accomplished when you reach that milestone? Who do you want to be?

Take time to deeply visualize the contents of this octave and write, draw, or otherwise illustrate what the fourth octave means to you.

The Fifth Octave: Power
Ages 52–65

The fifth octave begins at the Autumn Equinox and moves clockwise to Samhain. Once again, you may wish to reread the section on the octave in the last chapter before you consider the following questions:

- What power do you wield? What are you in charge of? How do you lead? Who answers to your authority and how do you wield that authority? Are you an expert or a senior partner in an enterprise? A parent or grandparent? A mentor?

- Who do you make decisions for and how do you use that power responsibly? How have the uses of your talents manifested as mastery in your field? Do you create or purge? Do you serve justice or mercy? Who do you have influence over? How do you use that influence positively?

If you are not yet in this octave or have not completed it, please consider the following:

- How do you want to do these things? What does the positive use of power mean to you? What would you do with power if you had it?

- How do you visualize yourself as an authority? Are you like or unlike the authorities in your life? What have you learned from others that shapes how you will wield power?

These are difficult questions. Each archetype wields power differently, and it may be helpful to consider different archetypes if you are having trouble visualizing yourself as a benign authority. The ruling queen is one that our society rarely portrays, though the king is often seen. Consider as well the master crafter, the scholar, and the scientist. There is the judge, the priest or priestess, father and mother. Imagine yourself becoming one of these leaders.

Then write or draw your thoughts in the octave, or otherwise record your musings.

The Sixth Octave: Wisdom
Ages 65-78

The sixth octave is the purview of the sage, of the wise woman and the wizard, of the hearty elder spilling riches from a cornucopia or the crone standing before the veil. If you are already in this octave, consider how you are embodying this story.

- Who are you guiding? What wisdom are you imparting? Do you teach compassion or do you render stern judgment? Are you standing apart as a wise hermit or are you the founder of the feast?

- What riches do you share? Knowledge? Material wealth? Opportunities? Experiences and the gathered wisdom of your long life? What are you doing that brings joy to others as well as to yourself?

If you are not yet in this octave, consider well-known characters who embody this octave.

- Are you Gandalf or Dumbledore? Baba Yaga? Isis of Amenti? Do you send the hero on their quest or are you the focus of the quest, the keeper of wisdom sought at great price? What do you want to be?

- Who fills this space in your life? Who do you know or have known in this octave and what has been their influence on you? How would you like to be like them or different?

- Lastly, what do you think it would feel like to be old? Our society is full of images of youth and of the illusion that physical frailty and signs of aging can be eradicated by using the right products or having the right lifestyle. Nevertheless, unless one dies young, everyone grows old. What does it feel like to hear that statement and to accept that fact? Imagine yourself old.

When you have taken sufficient time, record your impressions in the appropriate octave, either writing or drawing or in some other way.

The Seventh Octave: Death
Ages 78–91

If age challenges people in our society, death does even more so. We shy away from the idea of death, from the truth that sooner or later it is our fate. And yet it is inevitable. This octave is about accepting that.

Take a deep breath and prepare yourself. Then say aloud, "I am going to die." It's true. Perhaps (though it is unlikely) you will die tomorrow due to some accident or misfortune. More likely, you will die in old age as your body simply becomes increasingly frail and prone to illness. But you will die. Say it again. "I am going to die."

- Are you afraid? What do you fear? Do you fear the process itself or what comes after? What do you believe happens to consciousness, to the thing that is you, when you die?

- If you can, imagine your death. If you find this too upsetting, skip to the next paragraph. Who will be there? How do you hope that you will go? Do you want to die quickly, with barely a moment to understand what is happening? Do you want to die slowly, with time to say goodbyes and to prepare yourself? Do you want to postpone death as long as possible or avoid resuscitation and other prolonged medical procedures?

- Now imagine your memorial. Will you be buried or cremated? Will your remains stay at a permanent memorial? With a loved one? Be scattered? Who will pay tribute to you? What spiritual tradition, if any, will mark your passing? Who will mourn you?

- How will you be remembered? What will you leave behind of lasting value? What will be your legacy to people who knew you? What will be your legacy to the world at large? What do you want people to say about you when they remember you?

Write or draw your thoughts and responses in the octave. Take a long moment to consider what you have done and to ground any negative thoughts or feelings. You may wish to continue directly to the eighth octave, which is recommended.

The Eighth Octave: The Need to Be

Take a deep breath and center yourself. Close your eyes and consider.

Roughly a hundred years have passed since your birth. A number of years at least have passed since your death.

Who are you? Stripped of your name, your gender, your race, your ethnicity, your social identity, who are you? What is essential? What is the core of who you are?

"I need..." What do you need? Knowledge? Love? Service? Conflict? Exploration? What do you need, deep down at the core of yourself, deep in the earth?

You need something. And to have it, you need to be. You need consciousness and a body, to once again breathe and live in the light of the sun.

- Who do you want to be? Where do you want to be born? Who do you want to be your family? What circumstances will help you become what you most desire? Do you want to live in a particular place or among people with certain beliefs? Do you want a certain heritage or to experience life as a certain gender? Do you want a certain kind of physical body to achieve something in particular? Are there talents that you desire? What opportunities do you hope for? What is most important to you about the place in which you will find yourself?

- The future is not abstract. It is your future. You will live in the world we create. What do you want that future to be?

- Imagine yourself opening your eyes anew. What will you see? Where will you be? Who will nurture you? What will they teach you?

Hold that vision in your mind and write or draw in the octave before you. You have returned to the Spring Equinox, to the far right-hand side of the page; the wheel is complete and beautiful in its complexity.

You now have a map to your own personal Wheel of Life. Keep this project where you can see it. Update it as you walk through the years in and out of the octaves and as your desires change. Take a moment to be thankful for the Great Mystery. We dance the wheel.

····· **Chapter 4** ·····

Wheel of Time

During the course of our lives, if we live to old age, we will experience each season of the Great Wheel. However, the experiences of one generation vary remarkably from the experiences of another, because how we experience each season in large part depends on the interaction of the wheel of our lives with the greater wheel, the saeculum, the Great Wheel turning as we turn.

Visualize a carousel divided into four quadrants, each decorated with seasonal themes, each adorned with lights and decorations appropriate to spring, summer, autumn, or winter. If you are standing beside the carousel, you may see each season pass you in turn, an observer who is not part of its motion. However, the moment you step onto the carousel, you are in one season and one season alone. Your experience of the carousel is now limited—you are part of time, turning with the wheel rather than watching it from outside.

Thus, when a soul becomes incarnate, when you become a person, you are limited by your birthday. You are born at a certain point in the Great Wheel, in a certain season, and your perspective and experiences are then affected by this. Consider the example of World War II: Even if we control for other factors, and say that individuals A, B, and C are all white American middle class women born in a certain community, if one of them experienced World War II as the fifty-year-old mother of a young soldier, one of them as the twenty-seven-year-old woman who got a job in an airplane assembly plant, and the last as the nine-year-old daughter of a merchant sailor braving the Graveyard of the Atlantic, they would have radically different experiences! This is true even if they are the same gender, same race, same socioeconomic status, and all live in Baltimore! Their views of the war, the lessons they drew from it, the advantages and disadvantages it conferred on their lives—all these things would be different because of one simple thing—their birthdays. They stood at different points on the carousel.

Our place in the story is therefore a conjunction of two separate cycles, of two separate wheels, our Wheel of Life and the wheel of the saecula, the Great Wheel. In the previous chapters we explored the wheel of our lives. Now we will explore the Great Wheel and the great year of the saecula.

Mapping the Great Year

A great year, similar to the Wheel of the Year, is divided into the four seasons of Spring, Summer, Autumn, and Winter, which each last for about twenty years. These seasons follow one another in order, cycle after cycle. Sociologists Strauss and Howe call these seasons High, Awakening, Unraveling, and Crisis eras.[10] However, a Pagan view of this pattern easily relates them to the annual Wheel of the Year. To draw that comparison more closely, I am choosing to use the terms Spring, Summer, Autumn, and Winter, respectively, for the four parts of the cycle. These are capitalized to distinguish the saecular season from the annual season.

Returning to our original example in chapter one, the Etruscan village, the saeculum begins on the first day of its Spring, which is the day of the village's founding. Let's talk about who is present on that day.

First, there are the elders, the old people who have inspired this founding. While they may be few and are not doing the heavy work of building houses—piling up stones to make walls, digging clay and shaping it, and firing roof tiles—they are the ones whose lifelong work causes a new village to come to be. They are the ones who know how to found a town, the masters

---

10. William Strauss and Neil Howe, *The Fourth Turning*, Broadway Books, New York, NY, 1997

of crafts, the skilled midwives. Gray-haired pragmatists, they've picked the site and led people here. The priest who is dedicating this town represents them.

Second, there are the heroes, the settlers. Brave men and women in the prime of life, they're the ones who are doing the heavy lifting, both figuratively and literally. They're raising the cattle, raising the roofs, raising the children. They're plowing the fields and building the houses, making material progress to do practical things in a practical world. Most of the adult settlers are in this group.

Third, there are the children and young people. Ranging from two to twenty-two or so, these are the apprentices, the youths and maidens, the children who will grow up in this town. While they don't fully realize it yet, they will take the bare-bones structures their parents built and make them beautiful. They are the artists smoothing the edges and paving the streets with time for ornament and nuance.

Lastly, there is the baby. The youngest settler, he is the first of a new generation, the child who will grow up with peace and plenty and seek to change the status quo. Reform, revolution, awakening—all those tumultuous things are in the future on this founding day, the first day of Spring. Someday, he will be the old man, the last survivor of a generation of new ideas now absorbed into the society.

The baby is Spring-born, born at the beginning of the cycle. The priest is Summer-born, born fifty years ago in the last Summer. The baby's parents, the settlers, are Autumn-born, and the youths and maidens at the dedication are Winter-born. The seasons turn saeculum after saeculum, driven by the life cycles of the people.

The Summer-born priest and his generation are here because they are disaffected with where they grew up. Whatever city or town they came from, they wanted to leave. Perhaps they perceived insoluble problems. Perhaps they didn't like the way things were run. Perhaps it was too crowded or too poor. Perhaps there weren't enough resources to support everyone there, or perhaps an elite hoarded them. Whatever their reasons, they decided that the most practical solution was to just go. Self-reliant and fed up, they've voted with their feet and went off to found their own town. They nurture their children—the youngest adult settlers and the youths and maidens—carefully, determined that their kids are going to get a better start than they had and that they are going to have a better life.

The main body of settlers, the Autumn-born adults in their prime, think of themselves as heroes. They were raised to work together and to accomplish. Now as adults they are certain they can do whatever they set out to do. Found a new town? Sure. It's just a matter of allocating resources, making fair laws, working hard, and making sure everybody does their part. You can do anything with teamwork, perseverance, and good old elbow grease! As parents of the youngest youths and maidens, and of the baby and those that that will follow him in the next years, they're less protective than their parents. They believe children should learn how to think for themselves.

The Winter-born youths and maidens, raised to be helpful and productive, are beginning to dream things of their own. It's nice to put up a roof, but is it a good roof? If there was time, maybe some of these things that are purely functional could also be beautiful. And maybe these laws could be made fairer and more merciful. Maybe there's room for art and music, for depth and nuance, in addition to just getting it done. As parents themselves one day, they'll give their children the independence they themselves yearned for, even if that means going too far in the other direction and failing to protect them.

The Spring-born baby and those children who will come after him will be raised entirely in the new town. They will never know the old one with its flaws, but they will be all too keenly aware of the flaws in this one. Why do their parents make such a mess? Why is everything functional, philistine, and boring? Why are their parents so soulless, so focused on the here and now, so spiritually dead? As they become young adults, they'll challenge their parents' power by challenging their ideas. This will cause breakdowns at many points in society.

Meanwhile, in their shadow will rise a new group of hardy discontents who just want to start over, children who won't be born until twenty years after the town is founded.

Understanding the Great Wheel Today

Thus, like the Wheel of the Year, the Great Wheel is a movement between two poles. In the Wheel of the Year, these poles are winter and summer. In the Great Wheel, the poles are the Crisis era and the Awakening era.

A Crisis era, a Winter, ends with resolution, with a new beginning. Middle-aged pragmatists and young heroes have weathered the storm and start (re)building. Spring ends and Summer begins as the Spring-born reach adulthood, questioning the status quo their elders enacted and seeking to remake society. An Awakening era, Summer, begins when a society has reached a position of relative stability and prosperity but is also growing rigid and conformist. Disaffected young people rebel, and those who do not rebel grow more reactionary in response. The young separate into two camps that hold a real animus toward one another, unlike their elders who often see politics and culture as a genteel varsity sport and "agree to disagree." Autumn begins when the awakening burns itself out, with some new ideas adopted and some rejected, but most continuing to be a source of conflict in the society. As the years turn, the polarized factions grow larger and larger as the Spring-born generation claims power. Consider Puritans and Cavaliers, abolitionists and secessionists, or the Fascists and Communists of the 1930s—absolutes gain control of the dialogue. Society begins to break down and move toward a crisis as the competing values of the awakening fragment civil institutions.

Eventually, this reaches a tipping point and a new Crisis era ensues. Usually there is considerable bloodshed before one side or the other wins and their awakening values become enshrined. Gradually those values solidify, and in time a new awakening arises to challenge the status quo. Thus, the cycle is driven by the actions and relationships between the generations themselves. An extremely full and exhaustive analysis of these cycles can be found in William Strauss and Neil Howe's book *Generations*, which is highly recommended for those who wish to delve more deeply into the sociological theory behind this.[11]

11. William Strauss and Neil Howe, *Generations: The History of America's Future*, Morrow and Company, New York, NY, 1991

In other words, the season of your birth determines which of the classical stages of life you are in when you experience each season.

Generation	Childhood (Pueritia)	Youth (Iuventus)	Maturity (Virilitas)	Old Age (Senectia)
Spring-Born	Spring	Summer	Autumn	Winter
Summer-Born	Summer	Autumn	Winter	Spring
Autumn-Born	Autumn	Winter	Spring	Summer
Winter-Born	Winter	Spring	Summer	Autumn

Everyone will experience each season in order, but where you step on the Great Wheel determines how you, personally, experience each season. For example, if you are Winter-born, you will experience Spring as a young adult, while if you are Summer-born, you will experience it in old age.

The Problem of the Eternal Present

"When is your detective show set?"

"Oh, in the present."

We hear this a lot—"the present" as though it were some kind of endless moment, a setting apart from historical time. A detective show is set "in the present," meaning it's not in any historical moment. These fictional events don't happen on any "real" day. But of course they do. There is no such thing as "the present day." There are dates, and what date things happen on always matters because things are always changing. Sometimes the change is slow and sometimes it's swift, but change is constant. Ever go back and watch a show ten or fifteen years old that's set in "the present"? What the heck are those phones they're using? Seriously, they're using Netscape Navigator to look up information? And the cars—the cars look old instead of slick and new and hot. The present has moved on. Attitudes change, vocabulary changes, society changes.

History is not something that happened a long time ago. It's not something that happened before you were born. It's something that happened yesterday, in the moment that is already floating away from you down the stream of time. Tomorrow will not be like yesterday, perhaps in some small way, perhaps in a large one. A book set in Manhattan in June 2001 is not the same as a book set in Manhattan in October 2001. It matters which Manhattan you're writing about—pre- or post-9/11.

It matters in our lives as well. Did something happen in 2009 or 2010? Was it before or after your son was born? If you have a child, you know. Was it before or after your wife died? You know. Was it when you lived in Colorado or after you moved to New Mexico? Before you started college or when you were still in high school? Every moment takes place in history, whether that moment was two years ago or two thousand years ago. There is no "present day." The day these words were written is already far removed from the day you are reading them. They were written on a day that is now history.

Finding Your Place in History

However, we aren't taught to think about recent events as part of history. This exercise will help you place your own life in the context of history.

You will need a computer, tablet, or phone that will allow you to search the internet and a notebook or journal to take notes in.

First, do a search on the year you were fifteen. Maybe that was sixty years ago. Maybe it was one. Whenever it was, search on the year you were fifteen and consider the following questions.

- What were the most popular songs? What were the popular movies? What did fashion look like, not just high fashion but catalogs and advertisements? Did you wear things like this? Do you remember these songs? Which of these movies did you like and dislike?

- What was happening in the news? What were the major political issues of the day? What were the big pop culture stories? What were the scandals?

- What were the new technologies? What were the acceptable attitudes about gender, race, sex, and religion? Who did society approve of? Who did they disapprove of?

Make notes about what you discover.

Now do an internet search on the year you were born and consider these questions again.

- What were the most popular songs? What were the popular movies? What did fashion look like, not just high fashion but catalogs and advertisements?
- What was happening in the news? What were the major political issues of the day? What were the big pop culture stories? What were the scandals?
- What were the new technologies? What were the acceptable attitudes about gender, race, sex, and religion? Who did society approve of? Who did they disapprove of?
- What are the differences between your birth year and the year you were fifteen? How did things change? What new technologies emerged? What political issues came to the fore or were resolved and left the scene? How did attitudes change?

Make notes on these questions. Now do another internet search, this time on the year fifteen years before you were born.

- What were the most popular songs? What were the popular movies? What did fashion look like, not just high fashion but catalogs and advertisements?
- What was happening in the news? What were the major political issues of the day? What were the big pop culture stories? What were the scandals?
- What were the new technologies? What were the acceptable attitudes about gender, race, sex, and religion? Who did society approve of? Who did they disapprove of?
- What changed between that date and your earliest memories? What was the same? In what ways does the world of fifteen years before your birth feel like "history" rather than "the present day"?

The thirty years you have just searched, from fifteen years before your birth until fifteen years afterward, is a historical period. Write it down like this: 1953–1983, or whatever your years are. This is a specific historical period, just like the Victorian era or the Renaissance. This is the context of your life, the years leading to your birth and your formative years. If someone were writing a biography of you, this is where their story would have to begin, with the historical context for your life. It didn't happen in "the present" even if the years you've written down are 1988–2018. You were not born in "the present" and you didn't experience things in "the present." You are part of a specific period, a story that takes place in a certain historical moment, and everything you learned, saw, believed, were taught, and experienced happened through that lens.

The Great Year in the Modern United States

Next, we'll examine our own lives and our life stories in the context of the Great Story that is the history of our times. The following chart breaks down the seasons of the last saeculum and shows which generations were in which of the classical life stages at that point. It also gives a glimpse of the national mood at that time, a reflection of the season and its characteristics. If you are familiar with the work of sociologists Strauss and Howe and their generational theory, you will see how this takes the concepts that they address in *Generations: The History of America's Future* and applies those theories to the Pagan life cycle and Wheel of the Year. In other words, the four-part wheel has been broken out into the Pagan octaves and those octaves mapped onto recent history. This is an application of generational theory to a particularly Pagan understanding.

Our story begins with the Missionary Generation, born between 1865 and 1883. This was the Spring-born generation who were too young to have meaningful memories of the Civil War or slavery, and who came of age in the Victorian era. Stifled and overprotected, or isolated by poverty or by living in rural areas or insular ethnic neighborhoods of immigrants, they yearned for freedom and to change the big world by changing people's hearts. Ideas, from Marx to ecstatic Christianity and from Utopianism to Spiritualism, showed them maps to transform the world. Their coming of age, their Summer Solstice, was fraught with conflicts that dominated the rest of their saeculum, the great year just before the one we are in. Born in the era of corsets, some of them lived to see the era of the bikini.

They were followed by the Summer-born Lost Generation, born 1884–1904. The generation of doughboys and flappers, pieceworkers and bootleggers, they gave the Roaring Twenties its roar. They also made the twentieth century what it was, with writers like Hemingway, Fitzgerald, and Millay, the jazz greats, and the new entertainment center that touched across the globe: Hollywood. Most of the leadership in World War II were middle-aged Losties. Mostly born before the Wright brothers flew the first airplane, some of them lived to see the space shuttle launch.

The Autumn-born followed, the youthful heroes of the Greatest Generation, who won World War II and put a man on the moon. Born 1905–1925, they were also derided by their rising children as "the Man," influencing not only the saeculum they were born into, but setting the stage for the current saeculum as well. Today, the very oldest of this generation are fading away. In the next ten years all but a few thousand of this generation will be gone, the last GIs and Rosie the Riveters.[12]

The Winter-born Silent Generation (born 1926–1942) smoothed out the edges, a middle generation too young for World War II and too old to be hippies. They made their marks in the arts and sciences, contemporaries of Carl Sagan and Andy Warhol, Jane Goodall and Aretha Franklin, trying to perfect a complex postwar world. Today, they are the oldest generation living in any great numbers, and currently occupy the position of elders on the wheel.

The next cycle, the current saeculum, begins with the Spring-born Baby Boomers, born from 1943–1960. Recognized as a generation from infancy, they've driven trends from preschool onward. From the sixties and the Consciousness Revolution, to fundamentalism and libertarianism, they've remade the world with ideas, and the culture wars of the Baby Boomers remain the main conflict in the United States today, conflicts that remain unresolved well into this Winter. Most of the power positions in government, law, and culture are currently held by members of this generation.

They are followed by Summer-born Generation X, born 1961–1980, the slacker kids who, like Marty McFly, grew up to be fairly conscientious adults.

---

12. Niall McCarthy, "When Will the US Lose the Last of its World War II Veterans?" Forbes, May 28, 2018

Date	Octave	National Mood	Elders (Senectia)	Maturity (Virilitas)	Youth (Iuventus)	Childhood (Pueritia)
1940	Imbolc	grim	Missionary	Lost	Greatest	Silent
1950	Spring Equinox	resurgent and hopeful	Missionary and Lost	Lost and Greatest	Greatest and Silent	Silent and Baby Boomer
1960	Beltane	conformist and optimistic	Missionary and Lost	Greatest	Silent	Baby Boomer
1970	Summer Solstice	frenetic and free	Lost and Greatest	Greatest and Silent	Silent and Baby Boomer	Baby Boomer and Generation X
1980	Lammas	complex and challenged	Lost and Greatest	Silent	Baby Boomer	Generation X
1990	Autumn Equinox	fracturing	Greatest and Silent	Silent and Baby Boomer	Baby Boomer and Generation X	Generation X and Millennials
2000	Samhain	divided and darkening	Greatest and Silent	Baby Boomer	Generation X	Millennials
2010	Winter Solstice	moving toward crisis	Silent and Baby Boom	Baby Boomer and Generation X	Generation X and Millennials	Millennials and Homelanders

This generation was hit hardest by the great recession with the most lasting impact on lifelong earning potential, a generation of big winners and big losers. Now in midlife, Generation X composes the majority of workers, parents, and bosses.

The Autumn-born Millennial Generation is coming up fast behind. Born from 1982–2001, in 2020 they will eclipse the Baby Boomers as the largest generation of voters. Their large numbers and their civic-minded attitude mean they will be a force in public life long before they take the reins of power.

Finally, the youngest generation living today, the Homelanders, are the kids born in 2002 and since. They are still opening their eyes to the world, born in this current Winter, and their generational character will be established by the events of the early 2020s.[13]

We tend to assume that each generation is the parents of the next generation, but that's only half true. Each generation tends to be split between having parents of the previous generation and having parents of the generation two before. For example, a Millennial born in 1995 to parents thirty-nine years old has Baby Boomer parents, while a Millennial born in 1995 to parents twenty-five years old has Gen X parents. Also, often siblings span generational boundaries. If a Silent couple's first child is born in 1959, their second in 1962, and their third in 1965, the generational experience of their oldest and youngest is very different.

Numbers and birth years are all very well, but what does this have to do with lived human experience, especially since there are so many factors that make up one's life? We are part of the story, and the Great Story is made up of our combined stories. The history of the US is the history of us.

At this point you may say, "What if I'm not from the US? Why is this limited to US history?" The answer is very simple—the cycles are not the same everywhere in the world. Because each saeculum begins and ends with some important event, those beginning and end points are different for different people. A cataclysmic earthquake may nearly destroy one nation and have

---

13. Tim Elmore, "Homelanders: The Next Generation," *Psychology Today*, February 22, 2014

no impact whatsoever somewhere else. One people or one continent may be roiled by a massive war that countries across the globe do not participate in. The less contact and cultural influence there is between nations, the more their cycles do not run in tandem. For example, until the last forty years, contact between the US and China was quite limited. Of course there was trade but not a huge volume of it, and very few Americans visited China and Chinese visited the US. It's only in the last decades that Hollywood movies were ubiquitous in China and that Chinese students were common at US universities. Consequently, the US and China are on completely different cycles.

In a situation where there has long been a lot of contact and where many experiences are shared, the cycles are much closer together. Let's take the example of the US and France, where there has been a long relationship with much contact, travel, and trade. The cycles were fairly close together at the end of the eighteenth century. Our revolutionary era was from 1763–1783, while theirs kicked off in 1789 and lasted until 1815. Our Crisis eras were only one generation off. By the mid-nineteenth century, they were getting closer. Our mid-century crisis peaked with the Civil War from 1861–1865, while their Franco-Prussian War was 1870–1871. In the twentieth century, our cycles converged sharply. We both experienced World War II and the Cold War, and the cultural upheaval of the Awakening era touched us both at the same time, in 1968–69. It would be fair to say that at this point the French generational constellations and the American ones are very similar as a result of two centuries of entwined relations.

Because this pattern is different for every country and people, discussing the saeculum on a global scale is simply beyond the scope of a single book. This book focuses on the history of the United States and the way the Great Wheel presents itself in modern American society. If you do not live in the US, I encourage you to seek out works that deal with the cycles in other nations or to read on if you are interested in an insight into American life.

As you read the stories that follow, consider how they resemble or don't resemble your story or that of people you know. Consider how your story and your life fit into the Great Story of the saeculum.

····· Chapter 5 ·····
Spring-Born: 1943–1960

Valerie's Story

When Valerie arrived on campus at her state's flagship university in the fall of 1966, she was one of the first of an entirely new thing—a black coed. Until only a few years prior, the university had been segregated and only white students had been admitted. Then a few brave African Americans faced the discrimination and danger of being the first to break the color line and take advantage of new federal law that rendered discrimination in public education illegal. But at this university, they had been all men. Valerie's class was the first to include African American women.

In her plaid blouse with a Peter Pan collar and green poplin skirt, Valerie was the height of respectable fashion, a girl with brains and ambition who wasn't the least afraid of the challenges ahead. Valerie hoped that was the impression she was giving. It was the story she'd been raised to tell.

Born in the summer of 1948, Valerie was a beloved and much wanted victory baby, the name given to the Baby Boomers born in the immediate aftermath of the war. Like her brother, five years younger, Valerie was a child of hope. The hard times of the Depression and war were over. Her parents had both had difficult lives, her father overseas and her mother at home, and they had both lost people they loved. Those times were over. A new dawn had come, and Valerie was their victory.

Before she was four years old, they moved into a neat little brick house with three bedrooms and mid-century modern furniture. Her father was a funeral director (what, in the old days, would have been called an undertaker), a very respectable man, part scientist and part counselor. He was first to say in serious tones that embalming was a science and caring for the dead was a sacred trust. He was like a minister, Valerie thought, like a priest who served the gods of the underworld, helping families through the loss of a loved one.

Her mother no longer had to work. She was free to stay home with Valerie, lead a Girl Scout troop, and volunteer at school, in addition to keeping up all the community requirements expected of the funeral director's wife. Valerie was read to, taken to the library, parks, and playgrounds, and brought to church twice a week. All of these places were segregated, and in all of them she heard the same thing: You are the future of the community. You are the charmed child. You are beautiful and smart and valuable, one of the children that will lift us up. Our sacrifices and our parents' sacrifices will be rewarded in you, the best and the brightest.

A great struggle was happening. Everyone talked about it, a struggle for freedom that God himself demanded. Brown v. Board of Education required that schools be desegregated. Valerie was eight years old when her town complied. She walked into a mostly white school with her head held high, knowing that she carried her family's hopes and dreams. Her mother told her she had to be twice as good to get half the credit. "I'll be four times as good then," Valerie said, and she was. Her grades were straight As. She was the star reporter for the school newspaper and president of the community service club. She wasn't on the homecoming court and nobody with her skin color was, but Valerie didn't care much. What mattered was excellence, and her acceptance as one of the first black coeds at a flagship university mattered far more than some silly dance.

When she walked onto campus in the fall of 1966, it was with courage and confidence. Of course there were hardships and struggles, but justice and goodness always won. If she was worthy of the victory, she would win. Valerie intended to be a hero.

Four years later, by the day she graduated, May 7, 1970, the world had changed. Dr. King had been assassinated and so had Bobby Kennedy. Men had walked on the moon and thousands more had died in Vietnam. Just three days before her graduation, national guardsmen fired on student protesters at Kent State University, killing four. Valerie and her friends graduated with black armbands—those who attended at all. Her boyfriend didn't. He said graduation was for the establishment, for people who wanted to curry favor with powerful oppressors, with the Man. Instead, he joined a picket line outside the stadium, singing songs and daring the campus police to stop them.

Valerie didn't, and they had a huge fight about it. "My parents would be mortified," she said. "Besides, they've sacrificed so much so that I could graduate. They need to see me walk across that stage."

"Suit yourself," George snarled. "You go on pretending to be daddy's good little girl. It's not going to get you anywhere in this world. The time is over to be nice and ask for our rights. It's time to take them. It's time to throw a monkey wrench in the whole corporate/military establishment. This isn't about getting a degree so people will like you. This is revolution."

And yet she marched in her cap and gown. And yet she stood with her parents in the sun and her aunts took pictures of them with her diploma and her mortarboard and nobody said anything about the black armband, except her mother who sniffed. She didn't like it, but she didn't say a word. Her father hugged her and his eyes misted up as he stood beside his baby girl for a picture.

They all told Valerie how proud they were of her while she felt like a fraud. "I'm not," some part of her wanted to say, "I'm not your pure little girl. I've slept with my boyfriend and I don't go to church and I tried reefer at a party. I listen to Jimi Hendrix instead of Louis Armstrong and I don't wear panty hose under my blue jeans. And next week I'm moving in with George and we're not getting married. We'll be sharing a pad with three other people, and we're going to be part of a real community, a totally new thing. We're going to live communally and change everything. This is the beginning of a new age."

Midsummer, the Season of Fire

Valerie, born in 1948, is a first wave Baby Boomer. Born in the immediate aftermath of World War II, "victory babies" were the largest and most wanted generation America had ever known.[14] While vast inequalities remained, constant and consistent progress created an upward trajectory that seemed unstoppable. Better, stronger, brighter, clearer, fairer, cleaner, and more scientific—the world was improving every day, a tomorrowland of sanitary, air-conditioned houses and fast, shiny cars. Diseases that killed thousands were eradicated—polio, which had affected 35,000 American children in 1955, was reduced to 161 cases in just six years.[15]

Spring-born children like Valerie stepped onto the wheel just after the Spring Equinox, when each day dawned earlier and brighter than the one before, when warmth spread and the world greened. Problems could be solved by wise, fair adults. Heroes always won. Medicine could cure the sick, science explore the world, and justice perfect it even for those who had been long without. There was no target too high, no goal too impossible, not even the moon! When President Kennedy said that an American would walk there by the end of the decade, it was just a matter of making it happen with hard work, teamwork, and faith in science.

Valerie finished her first octave, passing from child to teen, in 1961. Her personal Beltane corresponded with that of the great year. The year 1961 was arguably the top of the American High and was the nation's Beltane as well as hers. This was the season of fire. Suddenly, for her and the country as a whole, there were new rhythms. There was the call of drums, the pulsing beat of blood, the first steps of a wild dance paced out in the screaming guitars of Woodstock and the thumping of helicopter rotors, blood and sex, and drugs and rock and roll.

Spring turned into Summer, the Summer of Love and the summer of death, Woodstock and the Tet Offensive, Apollo 11, and death at the Al-

---

14. William Strauss and Neil Howe, *Generations: The History of America's Future*, Morrow and Company, New York, NY, 1991

15. Sorem A. Sass and E.J. Gottfried, *Polio's Legacy*, University Press of America, Washington, DC, 1996

tamont Free Concert. Even as Neil Armstrong walked on the moon, a symbol of unity and progress, Spring-born children were dividing into eternal factions—flower children and national guardsmen, new agers and Jesus freaks, left and right culture warriors pursuing their own epiphanies, their own awakenings. The wars of first wave Baby Boomers against each other would define the next half century of American life.

Behind them, the second wave of Baby Boomers crashed into Summer more or less at the end of their first octave, a somewhat different experience.

Linda's Story

Linda was born on the island of Okinawa in Japan, an island far from her parents' native Puerto Rico, but she didn't remember it at all. Her father was in the navy, and in the summer of 1959, when she was a year old, he was reassigned to San Diego. California was the first home she remembered, California and the golden summer days of the early 1960s. By the time she was eleven, she lived in Chesapeake, Virginia. It was there, in the shag-carpeted den of one of dozens of nearly identical houses near the base that she watched Neil Armstrong walk on the moon, following every moment of the mission with bated breath. When at last the capsule reentered Earth's atmosphere, the long seconds of radio silence while the world waited to see if the astronauts would burn up or survive, she sat on the Naugahyde couch with her father's arm around her. "They'll be fine," he said. "Just a few seconds more."

Splashdown, and as the red and white parachute spread on the waves, he told her about the aircraft carrier waiting for them, the navy helicopters zooming in to pluck capsule and astronauts from the waves. "Those are our men," he said proudly. "I knew a lot of guys on the USS Hornet when I was stationed in San Diego."

"I want to do that," Linda said, watching the helicopter hover, the basket going down.

"Be an astronaut?"

"Be in the navy. Just like you, Papi."

Linda had two older sisters and she was her daddy's girl. She was the one who wanted to work on the car, who wanted to understand how everything worked, who wanted to take it apart and put it back together. They built a radio together when she was in middle school. In high school he took her on post (they lived in Pensacola then) and showed her how the radar worked, took her up in the main tower at the naval air station and introduced her to the controllers. She was fascinated, leaning over the controller's shoulder, watching planes navigating across the Gulf of Mexico, altitude and bearing and distance.

"Doesn't Linda have a boyfriend?" one of her mother's friends asked when she was a senior in high school.

"She's too busy for that now," her mother said easily. "There's plenty of time."

And she was too busy. There were a million things to do and never enough time to do them. Her senior year sped by, and before she knew it, she was walking across the stage to graduate from high school, the class of 1976. The valedictorian rattled on about not knowing what to do and finding a moral compass in these uncertain times and so on, but Linda barely listened. She knew what her future was. She had it all mapped out. Sixteen days after graduation, she reported for basic training for the US Navy.

———— • ————

The speakers were pumping out Blondie singing "The Tide Is High," and Linda was in a bar in San Diego with her friends. She was back in San Diego, but not as a kid this time. She had just made petty officer third class and she was out to celebrate. She was starting air traffic control training at Miramar. For the last half hour, a leggy blond woman in a sequined tank top had been sitting next to her at the bar drinking a Corona with lime. "You know there's another bar around the corner," the woman said. "We could go over there."

"Thanks, but I'm here with my friends," Linda said. There was something stunning about all this, something that was a lot headier than two beers.

The woman got up with a big smile, leaving her empty bottle on the bar. "Well, come on over if you change your mind." She leaned close, a whiff of

Chloe perfume. "You're awfully cute even if you're real butch." She walked away.

Linda stared after her. "What just happened?"

Her friend, Matthew, swiveled around on his bar stool. "She's a lesbian. She just made a pass at you."

Linda blinked. The woman was rapidly disappearing in the crowd, blond hair and tanned shoulders. "She thinks I'm a dyke?"

Matthew dropped his voice. Nobody else could have heard over the pounding music. "Well, you are, aren't you?"

For a second the world spun. It all made sense—her indifference to Matthew physically though he was her best friend, the guilty pleasure of watching women athletes excel, the heady moments of dancing on "girl's night out." And then reality. She'd just made petty officer. The navy would throw her out, a dishonorable discharge even if she did no more than admit to it, a discharge that would follow her everywhere in civilian life. Her career would be over before it had barely begun. And her parents—it was against God, against the teachings of the Church. She'd never be welcome at Mass again. Her father, oh God, her father! He would be ashamed of her where he had always been so proud. He was proud of her now, a great career, a worthy service.

She looked at Matthew evenly. "No," she said. "Absolutely not."

Lammas: Sacrifice and Harvest

Born in 1958, ten years younger than Valerie, Linda experienced the same moments in history very differently. For example, Linda did not remember John F. Kennedy's presidency or assassination at all. She was barely five years old when he died. An event that had a tremendous impact on older Baby Boomers meant little to her. Likewise, Woodstock and the Summer of Love meant much less to an eleven-year-old than to a twenty-one-year-old! Her touchstones were the late Summer days instead, the post-Watergate era of the late seventies and early eighties.

As a lesbian and a Latina, Linda faced different kinds of discrimination than Valerie did with very different impacts. The LGBT community of the late seventies and early eighties, in the pre-AIDS era, was a vibrant, sex-affirming scene—but one that came with a heavy price. In most parts of American society, being out and queer meant being a pariah. Doors closed, careers were off-limits, and outed parents could expect to lose custody of their children. Those in the armed services, like Linda, faced an even more onerous burden: the prospect of jail time if their sexual orientation became known. In thirteen states having sex with a consenting adult of the same gender was a felony, like possession of cocaine. To be LGBT and out meant to live in a subculture on the edges of society, and for women like Linda, to be butch or femme was a hard-won identity that defied gender constraints. Many people hesitated to come out because the price was so high.

And yet this period was one of growing freedom and pride in difference. For many people, the late seventies were a time of exploration, when boundaries were meant to be crossed and norms to be defied.

The days shorten though the heat endures. Leaves turn emerald, dark and overblown. Blackberries ripen on the vine. Thunderstorms roil the night sky, splitting the heat with wind and showers, gone the next morning. Everything was too ripe, too big, too hot, too lush. Change was coming. Summer was ending.

In the early 1980s, America's Summer ended. Autumn began.

Responding to the Spring-Born

Now we are going to explore our reactions to the stories and to the Spring-born in general. Whether you, yourself, are Spring-born or not, these exercises will help you put the generation in perspective.

For these exercises you may want a blank book or journal of some type so that you can draw or write your responses to the topics and questions raised. This should be a journal you are able to use throughout the rest of this book to do exercises and meditations. If you prefer to use a computer to record your thoughts, you can do so. Begin with the general questions, then follow the sections for Spring-born or not Spring-born as is appropriate to you.

If you are reading this book with other people and doing these exercises as a group, you may use these questions as discussion questions, and as starting points to share and compare your experiences. Remember, there are no right or wrong answers. Each person will have had different experiences and will stand at different positions on the wheel. Part of the purpose of these questions is to clarify what assumptions one has based on one's generational position and to better understand that others have very different assumptions based on their own position.

Valerie's Story

- What is your immediate emotional response to Valerie's story? Why do you think you feel that way?
- Do you identify with Valerie? With others in her life? How are you similar? How are you different? If you share some of the same experiences but were shaped differently by them, why do you think that was?
- What do you think will happen to Valerie next? Do you think Valerie is making wise or unwise decisions about her future? Why do you think that?
- Do you think Valerie is right to attend her graduation or not? Do you think she is right to wear the armband or not?
- What do you think of George and Valerie's relationship with him? What do you think of Valerie's parents and her relationship with them?

If you are also Spring-born (1943–1960), consider these questions:

- Are you older or younger than Valerie? Did you experience some of the same coming of age moments? How are your memories of those events different from hers? How are they the same?
- Does Valerie remind you of people you know? What has happened to those people in the years since then?
- Have you made some of the same decisions as Valerie? What happened to you as a result of those decisions? Have you faced the same decisions but made different choices? What happened as a result of those choices? If you stood before those choices again, what decisions would you make?

If you are not Spring-born, consider these questions:

- If you are old enough to remember some of the events of Valerie's life, how did you experience them differently than she does? How was your understanding or perspective different?

- Does Valerie remind you of people you have known, whether elders or juniors? How do you relate to those people?

- How is Valerie's experience different from yours because of her moment in time? For example, being in the class of 1970 is very different from being in the class of 1990. Are the expectations you had placed upon you as a young person similar or different? About work and school? About sexuality and relationships?

Linda's Story

- What is your immediate emotional response to Linda's story? Why do you feel that way?

- Do you identify with Linda? With others in her life? How are you similar? How are you different? If you share some of the same experiences but were shaped differently by them, why do you think that was?

- What do you think will happen to Linda next?

- Do you think Linda is making wise or unwise decisions about her future? Why do you think that? Do you think Linda is right to prioritize her career in the navy over her sexuality? Why or why not? What do you think of her decision to stay in the closet at this moment? Do you think she will change her mind later, or not?

- How do you think Linda's experiences are different from Valerie's because she is ten years younger? What opportunities and advantages are different? What disadvantages are also present?

If you are also Spring-born, consider these questions:

- Are you older or younger than Linda? Did you experience some of the same coming of age moments? How are your memories of those events different from hers? How are they the same?

- Does Linda remind you of people you know? What has happened to those people in the years since then?
- Have you made some of the same decisions as Linda? What happened to you as a result of those decisions? Have you faced the same decisions but made different choices? What happened as a result of those choices? If you stood before those choices again, what decisions would you make?

If you are not Spring-born, consider these questions:

- If you are old enough to remember some of the events of Linda's life, how did you experience them differently than she does? How was your understanding or perspective different?
- Does Linda remind you of people you have known, whether elders or juniors? How do you relate to those people?
- How are Linda's experiences different from yours or those of people you know because of her moment in time? For example, coming out as lesbian is a very different experience now than it was in 1980. How is Linda's experience as a lesbian shaped by her age?

····· Chapter 6 ·····

Summer-Born: 1961–1980

Jason's Story

Jason watched Neil Armstrong walk on the moon, but he didn't remember it. He was two months old. Born in April 1969, Jason mostly slept through the Summer of Love. His parents, Shirley and Hank, didn't listen to Jimi Hendrix or the Rolling Stones. They were Winter-born, children of the Great Depression, and their music was Chubby Checker, Fats Domino, and Elvis. Nobody wore love beads or peace signs at his house. His parents had been thirty-one when Jack Weinberg said, "Don't trust anyone over thirty."[16] His father sold insurance. His mother stayed home. Jason's older sister, Anne, was six years his senior, a perky grade school Brownie. Radical in his house meant watching the Brady Bunch, a blended family that wore bell-bottom jeans.

Everything changed in 1976. His father announced that he wanted a divorce. More than that, he was marrying his office assistant, Cynthia. He packed a suitcase and some cardboard boxes and moved out. A hush fell. It was like someone had died. The curtains were drawn. Everyone spoke in whispers. His mother's friends came and went with casseroles, sitting around the table in the darkened kitchen, whispering and whispering and whispering.

---

16. James Benet, "Growing Pains at UC," *San Francisco Chronicle*, November 15, 1964

Jason sat in the den and watched television. *Star Trek* was on in syndication, episode after episode, back to back. Jason stayed out of the way. Most of the time, nobody looked for him. They all had other things to do.

One month, two months. His father took him to McDonald's. He explained that he had a new apartment across town. He said a lot of things about how when two people grow apart, they find that they're no longer fulfilled, and that it's best if everyone moves on. "When are you coming home?" Jason asked.

"I have a new home now," his father said.

Three months, four months. His mother explained that they were moving too. Their house was going to be sold. Jason and Anne would go to different schools because they'd live in an apartment somewhere else. His mother was looking for a job. She'd never had one. She'd gotten married right out of college. She'd never gone to work or had a paycheck or anything, and jobs were hard to find if you were a woman over forty with no experience.

Three nights later, Jason heard a noise in the kitchen. He came downstairs to see his mother crying at the kitchen table, her head on Anne's shoulder. "Men are shit," she sobbed. "They're nothing but shit. Don't ever trust them. Don't ever believe them. All they want is one thing. You're a smart girl. You can do better. Stay away from boys, and never, ever waste your life having kids and keeping house."

"Yes, Mom," Anne said. Her face looked like she was in pain.

Jason tiptoed away. They didn't want him. And men were shit. Boys were shit. Kids were a waste of time. He got it.

———— • ————

The words crawled up the movie screen, crashing music echoing through every part of him. You could never see *Star Wars* too many times. Jason went to the dollar theater every weekend. His mom would drop him off on Saturday morning and he'd go with some guys, then hang around the mall and see it again in the afternoon. He knew every word. He knew every move. He wasn't some kid. He was Han Solo. He had the fastest hunk of junk in the galaxy, and he'd never let his friends down, not for a million bucks.

Anne got him a book for Christmas, which was weird, because he didn't read books. *"Han Solo at Star's End?"* he said, turning it over and freeing it from the wrapping paper beside the little artificial Christmas tree in Mom's apartment.

"It looked really cool," Anne said. She winked at him. "And it will help your reading." Sometimes he and Anne were still a team, even though she was a girl and everyone said you couldn't be friends with girls. There was something called the battle of the sexes, and it meant that boys and girls were enemies.

Actually, Jason was pretty good at reading. He was better at math. Math just made sense. Everything was orderly. But there was something even better than math, and that was computers. His high school had some, and in the fall of 1983 when he was fourteen, he took a class about teaching computers to do things by learning to program in their language. To his surprise, he got an A+. "I'm going to do that for a living," Jason said.

His mother looked confused. "That's a job?"

"I could make video games."

"Making games isn't a job."

His father didn't say anything about the report card. Cynthia had just had a baby, and he was really busy.

———— • ————

"Is this seat taken?" The reading room of the university library was almost full, every table packed with students studying for finals. The space opposite Jason was empty except for a pile of his books, and now someone wanted to sit down. "Hello? Is this seat taken?" He looked up and his jaw dropped.

Standing there with her backpack was a beautiful girl with her hair in one long braid down her back, a quizzical expression on her face. She was wearing a pink T-shirt with the outline of a head wearing side buns and the logo "This Princess Rescues Herself."

"Ah, no," Jason said. "I mean, nobody's there. I mean, that's my stuff. I'll move it." He jumped up, grabbing his books.

"Thanks." She plopped her backpack on the table. "I'm Jessica."

"Jason," Jason said. He hunted for something else to say, something clever and memorable. "Um, what department are you in?"

"Computer science." Jessica sat down and started unpacking.

"Me too." He gulped. How do you talk to a girl? He'd never had a girlfriend. He was a nerd.

But Jessica was easy to talk to. They were in some of the same classes. They'd seen all the same movies, read a lot of the same books. She loved *Star Trek II* but not *Star Trek III*, played *Traveller*, and was a top-notch player of *Beyond Castle Wolfenstein*. She even went to science fiction conventions. They talked until the library was closing.

As they walked out into the cool autumn night, Jason said as casually as he could, "I guess you wouldn't want to go out with me sometime?"

She turned to him with a brilliant smile. "And I guess you don't know everything about women."

Autumn Equinox: A Chill in the Air

Jason, born in 1969, is the middle of the baby bust, the generation which would be called Gen X. The social disruptions of the Summer, of the Awakening era, hit him in childhood rather than as a teen or young adult. Children were no longer wonderful darlings full of promise but hookers and demons, or at least burdens on an adult world that was absorbed with its own problems and personal passages.[17]

Stepping onto the wheel just after Midsummer, Jason walked into a confusing whirl, an adult party where elementary school children were supposed to learn about and grapple with adult topics from infidelity to the Holocaust. This was the era of the "latchkey child" who was supposed to supervise themselves after school, the streetwise smart-mouth who could handle it all. This was the era of the battle of the sexes, when antagonism between men and women was suddenly theorized to be a basic part of human experience, two creatures with nothing in common except the necessity to procreate.

---

17. Neil Howe and William Strauss, *13th Gen: Abort, Retry, Ignore, Fail?*, Vintage Press, New York, NY, 1993

Jason, like some of his peers, found both hope and community in genre media, in the company of friends who became his family. Other Gen Xers found other subcultures, but subculture community and the lateral bonds created were a hallmark of this new Lost Generation. Movies like *Ferris Bueller's Day Off* made it clear—the people you can count on are your friends.

The end of Jason's first octave, in 1982, corresponds with America's passage from Summer to Autumn. The freedoms which had seemed so alluring to like-aged Baby Boomers were now fraught with danger. The AIDS epidemic, seemingly coming out of nowhere, provided a new math: sex = death. The divorce epidemic meant that a far higher number of Gen X kids grew up in single-parent homes, and for the first time in fifty years, the poverty rate for children grew substantially.[18]

In the 1990s, as Jason and his peers reached young adulthood, the souring of the economy affected them disproportionally. For many Gen X kids who had been raised in the middle class, a middle-class lifestyle had became inaccessible. For those who had been raised in blue-collar families, it became nearly impossible.

And yet Autumn's days can be bright. In the Wheel of the Year, autumn has blue skies, temperatures moderated from summer's heat, the brilliant, fractured light through changing leaves—autumn can be glorious. For Jason and his peers, their second octave played out on a dangerous, heady playground as surreal as something out of a music video, frenetic, fascinating, and wildly unpredictable, a neon underground. It certainly wasn't safe, but it was fun—for the winners at least. And wasn't life divided into winners and losers? No second chances, no mercy—life is a winner-take-all gamble.

For the second wave of Gen X coming behind them, there had never been any Summer. They were Autumn's creatures.

Nikia's Story

To Nikia, Ronald Reagan had always been president. He had been elected when she was two years old, the same year that her father, George, split from

---

18. Jeff Leeds, "Child Poverty Grew in the 1980s," *Los Angeles Times, August 12,* 1992

her mother, Valerie. She didn't really remember George at all. He was a voice on the telephone calling on holidays. Her mom was the constant in her life.

Well, not that her mom was always there. Her mom worked long hours as a bank teller, and Nikia was at daycare until 5:30 or 6:00. Her daycare cost almost half what her mom made, Nikia heard her say once, but good quality daycare was a priority. Her mom hugged her and told her it was fair— they were a household of two, so half was for Nikia. She didn't question that at the time, not realizing that rent and food and power and all those other things came out of the other half. They were always there, and if her mother did without things, Nikia didn't notice. She was her mother's darling girl.

For a while they moved in with Stan and it looked like they were going to be a family, but Stan did something bad and there were women on the side, whatever that meant, so they moved back out of Stan's nice apartment into another small one, and nobody talked about Stan ever again.

Then Mom made an agreement with Grandma and Grandpa, and she was going back to school to get a masters in social work because Grandma said it would be tragic if Mom wasted her potential, which made Mom mad, but she didn't say anything because Grandma and Grandpa were giving her a lot of money. Grandma shook her head sadly. "You were going to be a hero," she said, looking around the apartment. "You had every opportunity."

That night after they left, Nikia climbed onto her mother's lap on the big black sofa. "Mom, why aren't you a hero?"

Her mom held her very tight. "Not every hero is famous, but every one is important. Have you ever heard the story about the starfish?" Nikia shook her head. "A woman was walking along the beach when she saw a starfish washed up on the shore. Now, starfish live in the ocean and they'll die if they're on land, so she picked up the starfish and carried it back to the sea and put it in the water and watched it go away. Then she turned around, and what do you suppose she saw?"

"What?" Nikia asked.

"The whole beach was covered with starfish. There were thousands of them. Ten thousand of them. More starfish than she could put back in her whole life, and most of them would die if they weren't back in the water in an hour."

"Oh, no!"

"And so she started picking up starfish and putting them in the water. Because even if she couldn't get them all, even one starfish is important." Valerie's arms tightened around Nikia. "Being a hero is picking up as many starfish as you can."

Nikia considered the story. "I would have helped her pick up starfish," she said."[19]

———— • ————

Her junior year in high school, Nikia had Mr. Simpson for Advanced Placement American History. He was a big man with a booming voice who made you want to sit still and listen, a way of telling you things so that they stuck in your mind, so that you felt like you were there when Lincoln read the Gettysburg Address or when Roosevelt said there was nothing to fear but fear itself. Nikia loved his class. It was full of ideas. One day in October of 1992, he had them read an article about a new book, about scholars saying that it was the end of history. "Is that true?" Mr. Simpson asked the class. "Do you think that competition between different points of view, different beliefs and religions and ideologies, is over? Do you think that the world is just going to get more and more homogenous, with cultural differences disappearing because of international corporations? Analyze and support your thesis in a three-page essay due Friday."[20]

Nikia worked hard. She finished her essay on Thursday night, eight pages instead of three, with eleven cited references. She ended on a personal note. "I am sixteen, and I don't know if this is the end of history. I don't know if everything I might do in my lifetime is pointless. But I do know this. I love the world being full of different things. I don't want everything to be just like

19. The story of the starfish has been retold in many essays by many different authors and speakers. The original story seems to be "The Star Thrower" by Loren Eisley in *An Unexpected Universe*, Harcourt Brace, New York, NY, 1969.

20. Francis Fukuyama, *The End of History*, Simon & Schuster, New York, NY, 1992

the town I live in. I don't want a melting pot. I want a patchwork quilt. That's why I want to be an anthropologist, so I can see the world and all different cultures before they disappear and everything becomes just like here. I want to save the stories even if everything else becomes McWorld."

The next week Nikia's mother was called in for a conference. "I swear I didn't do anything," Nikia said in the hall outside. Her mother had had to get off work early from Child Protective Services to come to the meeting right after school. "I don't know why Mr. Simpson wants to talk to you."

He opened the door. "Come in, please." He had chairs arranged around a study table and he pulled one out for her mother, who looked bemused for a minute before she sat down. "Nikia says you're a caseworker. I appreciate you taking time to meet today. I know that saving the lives of children in our community is very demanding."

Her mother put her head to the side. "Thank you. And I know that a good teacher is a rare gift."

"So is a rare student." Mr. Simpson sat down. He pulled out Nikia's essay, putting it in front of her mother with the big red A+ showing. "Nikia is an extraordinary student. She has an amazing mind coupled with an amazing heart—insightful and compassionate far beyond her years. I wanted to talk to you about nominating her for Presidential Classroom, a Washington, DC–based enrichment program for the gifted and talented. And also to discuss with you how I might help with her college applications. Nikia could go to a top-ranked school. Just let me know what I can do to help."

"Mr. Simpson..."

"Call me Leroy."

"Leroy. And I'm Valerie. I appreciate your offer so much. College admissions is a daunting process," Nikia's mother said. "While I'm absolutely in favor of Nikia doing enrichment programs, they're very expensive and I don't think that I..."

"There are scholarships," Mr. Simpson—Leroy—said. "I can nominate her for one. I have no doubt she would receive the maximum benefit from the program." He looked at Nikia. "A program in DC to study government and policy for a week during your senior year."

"I want to do it," Nikia said.

The next fall when Nikia went to DC, her mother and Mr. Simpson went with her for two days before so that she could combine her arrival with a college visit at American University. She was pretty sure it was her first choice, and by the end of the visit she was certain, American and a public policy degree.

She was also sure of something else, something kind of weird but good. When her mother and Mr. Simpson picked her up, they had something to tell her, standing together like they were afraid she would be mad. "Let me guess," Nikia said, pushing her long braids back, "You're getting married."

"How did you know?" her mom said.

"Just a guess," Nikia said, hugging them both tight. "I love you, Mom. I love you, Leroy."

———— • ————

Five years later, Nikia was interning at a DC nonprofit while she applied to graduate schools. It was a beautiful September morning. She was in the office early, listening to the voice mail and writing out messages for each of the senior staff, thirty-two voice mails about everything from development to programming. Nobody else was in the office yet, but their phones kept ringing. What was going on this morning? In the last few minutes, everybody's phone had been ringing off the hook.

Maybe there was a sound. She could never remember later if she'd heard it or not. Nikia looked up. Between buildings, down across the mall, a thick column of black smoke was rising. And then there were sirens. She left the receiver on the desk and ran to the window, leaning on the air conditioning vent to look out. Everything was very clear and very calm, as though suddenly life had shifted into ultrasharp focus.

Every emergency vehicle in the world was tearing down 19th Street. A hijacked plane had plunged into the Pentagon.

Nikia went home for Thanksgiving. That morning, helping her mom and Leroy make a sweet potato casserole, she took a deep breath. "Mom, there's something I need to tell you that you won't like." She felt her face heating. "I've decided that I'm not going to start grad school next year."

"Why not?" her mom sat down at the table. "I thought you were pretty confident of getting in."

"I am. But with everything going on in the world right now, I don't think I can do it. I don't think I can just go on to grad school like nothing's happening." Nikia took a deep breath. "I've enlisted in the army. I'm going to be a translator."

Samhain: Death and Dreams

The seasons of the Great Wheel are the seasons of our lives. The days shorten. Leaves that were bright orange and gold turn brown, tumbling from the trees to lie in great drifts. Nights are cold and clear with a beauty that pierces to the bone. Lights glow behind closed windows. It seems that spirits walk. Samhain is past, the dark fast approaching even as harvest feasts call us to gather together, seeking the comfort of one another against the gaining cold. Soon it will be Winter.

Winter's first storm was 9/11, blowing in on the wings of death. For Nikia, this began another phase of her life, when she newly dedicated herself to service and chose the role that she would play in the crises to come. Iraq, Afghanistan, and a darkening world full of new dangers that the optimistic globalists of the 1990s had not predicted became the new normal. For Nikia, this is her time, the first decades of the twenty-first century.

Responding to the Summer-Born

For the following journaling exercises, take out your blank book or notebook. If you are using a computer, turn it on. Remember, there are no right or wrong answers. Each person will have had different experiences and will stand at different positions on the wheel. In answering these questions, we are attempting to clarify what assumptions we have based on one's generational position, and to better understand that others have very different assumptions based on theirs.

Jason's Story

- What is your immediate emotional response to Jason's story? Why do you feel that way?

- Do you identify with Jason? With others in his life? How are you similar? How are you different? If you share some of the same experiences but were shaped differently by them, why do you think that was?

- What do you think will happen to Jason next? Do you think Jason is making wise or unwise decisions about his future? Why do you think that?

- What do you think of Jason's parents, Shirley and Hank? What do you think of his relationships with them?

- What do you think of Jason's experience of the sexual revolution, the sudden rise in the divorce rate, and the battle of the sexes? How might his experience have been different if he had been older? Younger?

- Are you surprised by Jason finding community in a genre media sub-culture? Is this familiar to you or unknown? Do you have feelings and prejudices about "fandom"?

If you are also Summer-born (1961–1980), consider these questions:

- Are you older or younger than Jason? Did you experience some of the same events or social trends? How are your memories of those events different from his? How are they the same?

- Does Jason remind you of people you know? What has happened to those people in the years since then?

- Have you made some of the same decisions as Jason? What happened to you as a result of those decisions? Have you faced the same decisions but made different choices? What happened as a result of those choices? If you stood before those choices again, what decisions would you make?

If you are not Summer-born, consider these questions:

- If you are old enough to remember some of the trends and social movements of Jason's life, how did you experience them differently than he does? How was your understanding or perspective different?

- Does Jason remind you of people you have known, whether elders or juniors? How do you relate to those people?

- How are Jason's experiences different from yours or those of people you know because of his moment in time? For example, Jason's experience of the sexual revolution is that of a child who experienced the maximum disruption. Was your experience similar or very different? How do you think this major social change impacted people you know?

Nikia's Story

- What is your immediate emotional response to Nikia's story? Why do you feel that way?

- Do you identify with Nikia? With others in her life? How are you similar? How are you different? If you share some of the same experiences but were shaped differently by them, why do you think that was?

- What do you think will happen to Nikia next? Do you think Nikia is making wise or unwise decisions about her future? Why do you think that?

- What do you think of what has happened with Nikia's mother, Valerie, who we met in Spring in Valerie's Story? Are you surprised by the trajectory of her life? Disappointed? Pleased?

- Do you think Valerie is a good parent to Nikia? Why or why not? What do you think of Leroy? What do you think will happen with Nikia's family in the future? Is Valerie a hero? Is Leroy? Is Nikia?

- What do you think of Nikia's experience of the sexual revolution? How might her experience have been different if she had been older? Younger?

If you are also Summer-born, consider these questions:

- Are you older or younger than Nikia? Did you experience some of the same events or social trends? How are your memories of those events different from hers? How are they the same?

- Does Nikia remind you of people you know? What has happened to those people in the years since then?

- Have you made some of the same decisions as Nikia? What happened to you as a result of those decisions? Have you faced the same decisions but made different choices? What happened as a result of those choices? If you stood before those choices again, what decisions would you make?

If you are not Summer-born, consider these questions:

- If you are old enough to remember some of the events and trends of Nikia's life, how did you experience them differently than she does? How was your understanding or perspective different?

- Does Nikia remind you of people you have known, whether elders or juniors? How do you relate to those people?

- How are Nikia's experiences different from yours or those of people you know because of her moment in time? How might your experiences be different if you were older or younger?

..... Chapter 7 .....

Autumn-Born: 1905–1924, 1981–2001

Daniel's Story

When Daniel was little, he loved airplanes. Sure, lots of kids born in 1990 did, but he loved even the ones that weren't "hot," big, passenger planes, even the giant UPS transport planes that landed on the runway like geese wallowing onto the surface of a pond. His mom and his dad took him on picnics out by the runway, which was kind of odd because they weren't together and never had been. They made jokes about turkey basters, which was really weird and maybe it was true because his dad was gay and his mom was a lesbian and they had both been out since before he was born. Once he asked them why they had him, and his mom had smiled, pushing her hair out of her face. "Josh and I are both Jews, and we both lost family members in the Holocaust. My grandparents—your great-grandparents—were killed. Josh's family was just down to his mother, the only survivor. And so family is really important to us. Even though we both knew we weren't going to get married, we wanted to have a Jewish child. It's what we owe our people. It's what we owe the future."

"So you decided to have me?"

His dad put his arm around Daniel. "Yep. We decided to co-parent you. And you are just about perfect."

His dad lived in another city seventy miles away with a guy named Steve who Daniel thought was his stepdad only that sounded like Steve and mom were an item. Daniel lived with his mom in the city, except on school breaks when he stayed with his dad. It wasn't that weird. Lots of kids had parents who were divorced. The only thing strange was that his parents had never been together. Nobody else had gay parents though.

His mom knew a lot of other gay people, and as a lawyer she volunteered for a center that helped gay people with legal issues. When he was just a little kid he already knew the difference between a medical power of attorney and a living will and could explain why you needed both so that if you were sick your partner would be able to make medical decisions for you and wouldn't be shut out of the hospital, like what had happened to a family friend, whose parents took him home to die of AIDS and his partner never saw him again. When his partner tried to see him, the parents had him arrested for trespassing. Mom told this story when she explained why you needed all these papers.

"So what happens to me if you die?" Daniel asked her.

She put her arm around him tightly. "First, I'm not HIV positive, so I'm not planning to die anytime soon, not until a long time after you're grown up. But if something did happen to me, my will says that you would go live with Dad and Steve."

"Because you don't have a partner."

"Danny, even if I did, she wouldn't have any legal rights." She hugged him again. "But it's ok. We live around the edges of the law, and I'm here to find the ways through. It's what Jews have always done, and what queers have always done, and we're all still here."

When Daniel was eight, one of the couples they had potlucks with had a baby. There was another kid with two moms! But she was a lot younger than him, eight whole years. "I can tell her how this stuff works," he said solemnly. "It's not easy being the only one."

For some reason his mom looked a little misty. "She won't be the only one. I know three more couples expecting. It's a gayby boom."

"Weird," Daniel said. Babies were not nearly as interesting to him as planes.

A few months later, somebody at school gave him a flyer and he rushed home with it. "Mom! We have to do this!"

"Do what?" She examined the flyer, a frown on her face. "Kids Day at the Base? Kids fourteen and younger can tour the airbase, see the planes and tower, and meet the pilots?" She shook her head. "Oh Danny, no. This is the navy base. This is military stuff. We don't do military stuff."

"But it says kids can see the planes!"

"The navy hates gay people. The navy hates liberals. We can't visit the navy base."

She really didn't understand how important this was. And he was getting mad. Surely, at nine years old, he was old enough to have something in his life that wasn't about her being gay. "Mom, how are they going to know you're a lesbian? You don't walk around with it written on your head! This is not about you."

For a second she recoiled, and then her face changed, a kind of stiff smile that showed she was trying. "You're right, Danny. This isn't about me. You do lots of things that are about me."

"You think I like going to all these potlucks with women who talk about knitting all the time?" He tried to make it funny, but it wasn't. "Because you don't think I'll be welcome anywhere else? I'm not good enough to do soccer or boy enough to do whatever?"

Now she looked sad. "No, Danny. I think I won't be welcome any of those places." She took a deep breath. "But it's not right for me to keep you back from having normal activities because they're not gay-friendly. You're probably not gay." Mom smiled, even if it looked a little forced. "Ok. We'll go visit the base and you can look at the planes. I'll be your tagalong this time."

"Awesome!" Daniel jumped up in the air. "You wait. It will be the best thing ever."

It pretty nearly was. They toured the flight line with a big group of mostly boys and mostly dads, though nobody seemed to think it was weird he had his mom instead of his dad with him. They saw F-15s and F-16s, transport planes and a rescue helicopter. They got to go inside the rescue helicopter and a rescue diver told them how he was trained to dive in and get a drowning person aboard. It was very cool.

Then they went to the control tower. The chief petty officer showing them around was a woman, short and dark-skinned with hair cut like a man's and a white uniform. She showed Daniel the equipment, taking lots of time with him and Mom. And Mom was really trying. She was making conversation while Daniel sat in the chair with headphones on, listening to the chatter between aircraft and the other controllers.

He caught something about "... oh no, I'm a single mother. By choice."

Now another controller was talking to a training flight out over the ocean, warning them to avoid a passenger plane on approach to the civil airport. Daniel could hear every word of it. It was indeed totally awesome.

About a week later he was doing his homework while his mom hopped around the apartment cleaning like crazy. Then the doorbell rang. It was the chief petty officer from the base, only she was wearing jeans and a leather jacket and looking nervous.

"Hi!" his mom said in a really high-pitched tone. She had on nice clothes and nail polish. "I'm sorry the sitter's not here yet, but you know Daniel."

Daniel got up. "You're going out?"

"Just to grab a bite of dinner." Mom had that deer-in-the-headlights expression.

The woman shook his hand like he was a grown man she was meeting. "You can call me Linda."

"I'm still Daniel," he said. And then he got it. "But you'd better be real careful of my mom and treat her right."

Linda didn't laugh. "I'll do that," she said. "Your mom is really special."

After that Linda became a regular fixture in their lives. All through the fall and winter she was around a lot. For his birthday she took him to the amusement park, just the three of them, and she went on all the rides with him that his mom said were too dangerous. "Come on, Rachel," she said. "Look at all the other kids. He's turning ten. He's old enough to be challenged a little if he wants to be." And so he and Linda went on the big coaster and the other hot rides and she didn't try to hug him or ask if he was ok. She just assumed he was.

Sometimes in the spring she even picked him up at school when his mom was stuck in court because her case was really low on the docket. She couldn't come in and get him, but he'd run out to her car. She had a Mustang, a real muscle car, and it was a lot hotter than Mom's Camry. By the beginning of summer, she stayed over at night too, and that was ok. She made a mean potato pancake. It was, Daniel thought, a lot like having a dad.

But sometimes Linda and Mom argued. "I can't go to Pride, Rach! You know I can't. Don't Ask, Don't Tell. I'm fine as long as I'm discreet, but Pride is out."

"You mean you're not out." Mom's voice was brittle. "Fine."

"As long as I don't flaunt it ..." Linda began, but Mom had already walked away.

Daniel figured it was time to take things into his own hands. The next time Linda picked him up after school he slid into the front seat with a plan. "Look," he said. "I'd like you to be my dad. Or other mom. Or whatever. But there's something you have to understand about Mom."

"What?" she swiveled around in the seat, the car still at the curb.

Daniel was firm. "She works for the community, and the community is everything to her. It's her home, and people rely on her to keep them safe, to help them when they're in the hospital and to help them have kids with donors and to make sure people don't lock them up or take away their kids in custody battles. She's a leader. This is what she does. Just like you keep people in airplanes safe. That's what you said: it's a calling. You keep people from dying in plane crashes. Mom keeps people from dying alone. She's not going to give that up or go in the closet for you. It would break her heart to say goodbye to you, and I would cry a lot too, but she's not going in the closet. Ever. So you need to figure out if you're going to come out and be a family or walk away."

Linda looked stunned. "Daniel, I ..." She took a deep breath. "But like you said, keeping people safe in the air is what I do. I can't give that up either."

"Do you have to be in the navy to be an air traffic controller?"

Her face changed. "No." She was quiet a minute. "Twenty-two years. Maybe that's enough."

So Linda retired from the navy and she got a job at the airport in the control tower there. He started middle school, and he and his mom and Linda moved into a house they bought in an older neighborhood that was getting some young people again. Daniel's grades were great and he went out for the soccer team and if anybody said anything when he played away games and both Mom and Linda came, he just stared them down. It was their problem, not his.

———— • ————

One morning he woke up to the television blaring in the living room and Linda rushing off to work two hours early. Daniel wandered in rubbing his eyes. His mom was crying in front of the TV set. "What happened?" he asked.

"Someone deliberately crashed two planes into the World Trade Center," his mom said, not taking her eyes off the screen where towers bled plumes of smoke into the clear morning sky. "We don't know who or why. But they're using planes as weapons."

"Where's Linda?"

"They called her in early. Nobody knows who's responsible or what happened."

Daniel came around and sat down beside her on the couch. It wasn't a movie. It was real. Something seismic had shifted, but that wasn't unexpected. That was what happened in books when the hero was old enough. Dragons attacked or Voldemort returned or aliens took over the world. It was time. It was his time. He put his arm around her. "Don't worry, Mom," he said. "I'll take care of you."

Winter Solstice: Gather Together against the Dark

Daniel, born in 1990, is in about the middle of the generation called the Millennials, and at the very beginning of the "gayby boom." While LGBT people had always had children through heterosexual relationships, deliberately conceiving children in a queer relationship was extremely rare for both legal and practical reasons. In the 1990s those barriers eased, leading to what was dubbed the "gayby boom," a sudden increase in the number of children born into same-sex partnered families. Of course this came with many challenges, including legal rights to custody, second-parent adoption as a means of establishing a legal relationship between a non-biological parent and a child, and many other legal challenges around fertility and conception. Kids like Daniel, born early in the boom, also had the added fear of HIV. In a time when it was conventional wisdom that all queer people would contract HIV and die young, even though that was never true, the fear of being left an orphan was very real for many.

While his experience in this way is unusual, in other ways Daniel is very typical of his generation. The Crisis era began when he was in middle school, and he cannot remember a time before he was at the epicenter of the culture war. By the time he was twenty-five, the war in Afghanistan had gone on for nearly half his life. His is the generation of Harry Potter, when kids save the world because adults are powerless or foolish. His is the generation of the Lord of the Rings, when even the smallest people can make a difference.

Having graduated from high school in 2008, college in 2012, and medical school in 2016, Daniel eats avocado toast and knows the world depends on him. Fortunately, he's pretty sure that he and his friends are up to the challenge. After all, aren't the kids supposed to save the world?

In a moment, Autumn turned to Winter. The last leaves were scoured from the trees, and with a blast of wind, Winter blew in on the wings of storm. The Crisis era has begun.

Charles's Story

The first thing Charles remembered was the sound of trains. They wove through his dreams, the clickety-clack of wheels going across the trestle, the long whistles as they slowed down for the crossings, the hiss of brakes as they started braking for the station five blocks away. He was born in a four-room wooden house near the tracks in the spring of 1923, and his father was a Pullman porter.

Charles loved trains. He knew all the numbers and schedules, and he could tell the difference in sound between the long freight trains, the locals, and the express passenger trains that whisked people away to unspeakably far destinations: Chicago, New Orleans, Atlanta, New York. One day he was going to go to all those places.

They had a radio, bought with the extra money his mother made doing laundry for the hospital, and on clear nights they could pull in stations from far-away places, his father tuning the set carefully until a wash of sound brought in jazz or big bands. "That's Cab Calloway," his father said, as Charles listened open-mouthed. "And he's as black as you or me."

"And he's on the radio?" Charles said, listening to Calloway's smooth patter.

"He's on the radio because he's that good," his father said. "White folks listen to him too."

And that was a wonder. There was an unspoken line down the railroad tracks. Whites lived on one side, blacks on the other. You crossed over to work, but you didn't stay. Only sometimes the line blurred. One time Charles asked his mother why he didn't have little brothers and sisters like most of his friends did. His mother looked up from the shirts she was ironing for his father. "I had some trouble when you were born," she said. "Bad trouble. What they call *placenta abruptio*. I'd have bled to death and you'd have died if a white doctor hadn't operated on me. He took my whole uterus out, so I can't have any more babies. Operated on me right there, in the white hospital where I work."

Charles frowned. "It doesn't seem right that you can't have more babies."

His mother put her arms around him. "He saved my life and my son. Jesus put him there to save you and me. That's more than anybody could pray for. You're our only child, and we don't need another." Charles folded up in his mother's arms. Her love was steady and strong, and Jesus's must be too.

Sure, there were bad things going on in the world. There were gangsters and crimes and kidnappings and problems with something called the stock market. They were in what grown-ups called the Great Depression, and somewhere people's farms were blowing away, but not here.

One day he got home from school and his father was already there. Charles stared at him. "Why are you here, Pop?" His father just walked out on the back porch without saying a word.

"He's been laid off," his mother said. "The railroad doesn't have as many passengers as it used to have, and most of them are riding coach instead of in the more expensive Pullman cars. They don't need as many porters." She put her hand on Charles's shoulder, though she was still looking out the back screen door. "Don't worry, Charles. I have my job at the hospital."

Her job didn't pay much, not nearly as much as they needed, and his father couldn't find anything permanent. He worked at a lumber yard for a while until winter came and people stopped building houses. He worked for the coal company making deliveries until spring came. Then he didn't have anything for a long time, and Charles's pants got too tight and his sleeves too short. Then he had a job shoveling gravel for the railroad to repair the grade until it was finished. Then he repaired the street. And then there was nothing again. He stayed out late and sometimes didn't come in until morning. One morning there was a knock on the door while Charles was eating breakfast and reading the funny paper. He didn't even look up when his mother went to answer it, only when he heard her scream.

His father had been hit by the 3:02 inbound to the railyard. He must have been walking on the track. Why he didn't get off when he heard the train, "it wasn't moving that fast, ma'am …" His father knew the schedules. He knew there'd be a train then, and it was dark and there was a curve. The engineer couldn't see him, but he must have heard the whistle for the Patterson St. crossing.

All that went through Charles's mind then and later, but nobody ever said the word. Nobody ever said suicide. His mother never said it. She just looked old in that one day. The minister shook his hand rather than hugged him. "You have a fine young man here," he said. "Charles, I know you'll be a comfort and a prop to your mother."

"I will, sir," Charles replied. He was the man of the house now. He was twelve years old.

He got a job selling newspapers on the platform after school when the evening trains came in. "Just one dime! Just one dime, sir, for all the latest!" He found that he sold best when he could say a little bit about what was in the paper, and so he read it all in the breaks when there was no arrival or departure. "Lindbergh kidnapper executed!" "Haile Selassie asks League of Nations to condemn Mussolini!" "Hitler annexes Austria!" "Prime Minister promises 'peace in our time'!" The world was a dark place and it was getting darker every day, an inexorable turn to the bad.

But that wasn't what the comics said, what the movies said. It wasn't what Superman said. "In such times, heroes are made." Charles was a hero just waiting for the call all through those years, all through the long years from twelve to eighteen.

———— • ————

It came on December 7, 1941. The Japanese bombed Pearl Harbor. The next day the United States declared war. He was eighteen years old, driving a truck for the lumber company. His mother cried when he told her what he was going to do. "Mama, if I'm going to drive a truck, I can drive it just as well for the US Army as anybody else."

And drive a truck he did. He drove it all over the eastern US. Then he got sent to England and he drove a truck there, up and down country lanes and through the fen country, carrying bombs and bacon and letters from home to hidden airfields where Spitfires and Mustangs rose to fight the Luftwaffe. He was a link in the chain, one part of a mighty machine that was going to save the world.

His buddy was Al, a big guy who was as loud as Charles was quiet, as brawny as Charles was slight. One day he taped a picture to the dashboard, a smiling girl with enormous, sooty eyes and an expression that made you think her soul was shining through her body. "Is that your girlfriend?" Charles asked. She was the most beautiful woman he'd ever seen.

Al gave him a shove. "That's my sister, man. My twin, Albertine. Albert and Albertine. So don't you go getting fresh."

"I wouldn't do that," Charles said. He wasn't the type.

Albertine's picture stayed on the dash when they went to France. The Red Ball Express followed the invasion forces, bringing up food and ammunition and medical supplies and everything else they needed, driving straight from Eisenhower's artificial docks and then from Le Havre to where the fighting was.

They were almost to Aachen when a Stuka dive bomber dove on the convoy. Charles heard the scream of its dive like a train whistle and time elongated, the deadly shape of the Stuka, the bright fire of its tracers as it went straight up the highway, two-ton trucks in a line with nowhere to go. Al swore, pulling hard to the left as the truck ahead suddenly slammed on brakes. Charles could never remember which happened first, the collision with the back of the other truck, front-passenger side hitting head on, or the Stuka's bullet smashing the windshield and going straight through Al's head. It was all one blinding moment.

In the hospital they said he was lucky. He had a broken leg and a broken foot. "I've seen a lot worse," the doctor said with what was supposed to be reassurance. "You'll walk again. Just need some time. I'm going to send you to the hospital in England. A couple months and you'll be A-OK." He turned to leave, then stopped as if he'd remembered something. "Oh. The medic who pulled you out grabbed this. Reckon it's yours." He handed him Albertine's picture. There wasn't a stain on it.

The hospital was very nice and everyone treated him right, even the English nurses who were white, but he had to get back to the front. The war had bogged down at the Rhine and winter was coming. His leg and foot were in a cast, and then he got the cast off and a brace instead and a lot of exercises for physical therapy. The Germans had launched an offensive right before Christmas and he caught the C.O. in the greenery-bedecked hall of the great house they were using for convalescents. "Sir, I want to know when I can rejoin my unit."

The C.O. frowned. "I'm not sure you're going to. Your leg's healing nicely, but you don't have the full range of motion or strength in that right foot. I don't think you're up to driving ten hours a day anytime soon."

Charles swallowed. "I'd like to volunteer for a combat unit." Al was dead. It was time to do something.

The C.O.'s face softened. "They're not going to take you in a combat unit with a bad foot. It's too much of a risk to everybody else to have a man who's not in top shape. I think you're probably getting a ticket home soon."

"I don't want…" Charles blurted. Then he stopped and made himself say it diplomatically. "I can't go home, sir. Not when there's work to do. Not when my buddies…" He stopped again. "Isn't there anything I can do over here where my foot doesn't matter? I could volunteer for mortuary duty."

The man's expression was kind. "Son, nobody volunteers for mortuary duty."

"I do," Charles said.

He was in Germany four weeks later, hunting bodies from the Battle of the Bulge. It had been a huge battle over miles and miles of forest, the snow sweeping in to cover all. Now they were looking for the bodies. Weeks, the elements, and animals had taken their toll, not to mention combat. Sometimes they found little. Sometimes they found parts, sometimes corpses that must be carefully examined, personal possessions logged, dog tags checked, and personal items boxed neatly and labeled to go home while the thing that had been a man went in a government-issue body bag. The job was every bit as grim as you would think.

And yet, sometimes while he carefully removed an undamaged wrist-watch from a cold and frozen wrist, he felt the man behind him, heard him like a spirit bending near. *It's ok, brother,* Charles said in his mind. *I've come to take you home. You are not forgotten. I will make sure your wife gets this watch and the picture of that baby girl. I will make sure your last letter you never finished gets to her. I will lay you to rest with your brothers in holy ground. I will be your priest.* Sometimes it came to that, when there wasn't a chaplain around. Charles spoke the Lord's Prayer from memory, and that bit from Ecclesiastes he liked, "To everything there is a season…"

Winter turned to spring. Berlin fell. Charles followed the army, burying bodies. Spring turned to summer. Their job was retracing steps, talking to people in France or Belgium who might have buried American servicemen in their country churchyards or their pastures. Charles tramped through the hedgerows with an elderly Frenchman who showed him where he'd buried the crew of a bomber, each shrouded in his silk parachute, hidden by night so the Germans wouldn't find them. Charles was there to exhume them, get their ID established, and make sure they were reburied with full honors in a military cemetery. The Frenchman smoked a pipe. "Don't you have a home to go to?" he asked.

"I'll go when the work is done," Charles said.

It was November when he got home. The war was over. His mother was small and gray and the town was small and gray. He talked to the local mortician. "I want to be an undertaker," he said. "And yes, before you tell me, I understand."

But there was one more thing to do. The week before Christmas he hopped on the train, watched it wind its way through familiar countryside to the unfamiliar, the cities that had once seemed so distant now so much closer than Belgium or France. Going to the city was no big deal. He got a cab to the address he remembered. It was a little brownstone, lights on inside, a wreath on the door, a flag with one gold star in the window. He knocked. She opened the door.

"You don't know me," he said. "My name is Charles. I was a friend of your brother's."

"Please come in," Albertine said, her luminous eyes suddenly full of tears. Charles knew in that moment he would make them smile again.

Imbolc: The World Ends and Then Begins Again

Charles, born in 1923, is in the last cohort of what would come to be called the Greatest Generation. This is also the group of children hit hardest by the Great Depression. Too young to fend for themselves and too old to be helped in childhood by the poverty relief efforts that were underway by the late 1930s, they had the highest child poverty rate ever recorded across all races and regions. They had Prohibition and bootleggers, celebrity kidnappings and gangsters, social violence and violence abroad, coming of age amid what were widely perceived to be rapidly worsening conditions. Pundits gloomily predicted a generation of failures, heirs to less and less, in a world painted as Gotham by detective comics and film noir.

Instead, they cast themselves as heroes. Male and female alike, they volunteered for social action, building dams and roads and airports with the Civilian Conservation Corps and the Public Works Administration, creating public art and recording folk narratives of history that would otherwise be lost. They became the Rosie the Riveters and G.I. Joes of the Second World War, building ships and planes and using them to defeat the Axis powers. Arguably, they set out to save the world. Arguably, they did. At the very least, they stopped Fascism for sixty years. They built a postwar world of previously unimaginable wealth and stability.

Even African American GIs like Charles found opportunities opening up that didn't exist in his childhood. Mortuary school, to learn the profession of undertaker, was paid for by his GI Bill, post-secondary education that would have been unthinkable a generation earlier. By the time his daughter, Valerie, and his son, Albert, were born, Albertine could stay home with them, Charles's income allowing them a comfortable life in a new house with all the modern comforts: indoor plumbing, refrigeration, air conditioning, and even, by 1960, a washing machine and dryer!

If their culture seemed a little staid compared to the electric Harlem Renaissance or the bad-boy lyrics of Cab Calloway, they liked it that way. The world was getting better. It was getting cleaner and fairer and more rational all the time. Who could yearn for Autumn in Spring?

Their children's rebellions in the 1960s took them by surprise. By the time Charles attended Valerie's graduation in 1970, he had no idea why the world was changing again.

Responding to the Autumn-Born

Once again, take out your blank book or notebook for journaling. Turn on the computer if that is what you have been using. Remember, there are no right or wrong answers. We all understand the world from our own point on the Great Wheel.

Daniel's Story

- What is your immediate emotional response to Daniel's story? Why do you feel that way?

- Do you identify with Daniel? With others in his life? How are you similar? How are you different? If you share some of the same experiences but were shaped differently by them, why do you think that was? What do you think will happen to Daniel next?

- What do you think of what has happened with Linda, who we met in Spring in Linda's Story? Are you surprised by the trajectory of her life? Disappointed? Pleased?

- Do you think Rachel is a good parent to Daniel? Why or why not? Do you think Linda is? What do you think of Rachel's community and her place in it? Do you have experience with the LGBT+ community yourself? How are your experiences similar or different? How much do you think Rachel's world in the 1990s is shaped by the AIDS epidemic?

- What do you think of Daniel's experience as one of the first children of the "gayby boom"? How might his experience have been different if he had been older? Younger?

If you are also Autumn-born (1981–2001), consider these questions:

- Are you older or younger than Daniel? Did you experience some of the same events or social trends? How are your memories of those events different from his? How are they the same?

- Does Daniel remind you of people you know? What has happened to those people in the years since then?

- Have you made some of the same decisions as Daniel? What happened to you as a result of those decisions? Have you faced the same decisions but made different choices? What happened as a result of those choices? If you stood before those choices again, what decisions would you make?

If you are not Autumn-born, consider these questions:

- If you are old enough to remember some of the events and trends of Daniel's life, how did you experience them differently than he does? How was your understanding or perspective different?

- Does Daniel remind you of people you have known, whether elders or juniors? How do you relate to those people?

- How are Daniel's experiences different from yours or those of people you know because of his moment in time? How might your experiences be different if you were older or younger?

Charles's Story

- What is your immediate emotional response to Charles's story? Why do you feel that way?

- Do you identify with Charles? With others in his life? How are you similar? How are you different? If you share some of the same experiences but were shaped differently by them, why do you think that was?

- What do you think of Charles's parents? What do you think of his relationships with them? Do you think his father committed suicide or not?

- What do you think of Charles's experience of growing up African American in the 1920s and 1930s? How might his experience have been different if he had been older? Younger?

- Are you surprised by Charles's finding a vocation as an undertaker? How do you feel about his military service and his relationship with the dead?

- Knowing that Charles and Albertine will become Valerie's parents in the Spring-born chapter, how does knowing Charles's story alter your viewpoint on them in that chapter? How does it alter your viewpoint on them in Nikia's Story?

- Does Charles remind you of people you knew? What has happened to those people in later years?

If you are Autumn-born in the next cycle (1981–2001), consider these questions:

- Have you experienced some of the same social trends or experiences as Charles even though you live in a different era? How are those experiences the same or different?
- Have you made some of the same decisions as Charles? What happened to you as a result of those decisions? Have you faced the same decisions but made different choices? What happened as a result of those choices? If you stood before those choices again, what decisions would you make?

If you are not Autumn-born, consider these questions:

- If you are old enough to remember some of the trends and social movements of Charles's life, how did you experience them differently than he does? How was your understanding or perspective different?
- Does Charles remind you of people you have known, whether elders or juniors? How do you relate to those people?
- How are Charles's experiences different from yours or those of people you know because of his moment in time?

..... Chapter 8 .....

Winter-Born
1925–1942, 2002–?

Shirley's Story

The first thing Shirley remembered was the big white house. Her parents had moved there just before she was born, in the summer of 1936, and she'd heard the story a million times. "I was working with this guy named Bob Patterson," Daddy would say. "He wasn't a great salesman."

"Not like you, Daddy."

"That's right. Not like me." He would lift her onto his lap in the green chair, careful of her starched petticoat, and put his arm around her. "So Bob came in one day and he was distraught."

"What does distraught mean?"

"It means very upset, toots. Now let me tell the story." Her daddy smelled like pipe tobacco and Old Spice, and he could tell the best stories. "Seemed as though he was buying this big house on time and he couldn't make the payments, so the bank was going to foreclose. He'd be ruined then, sure as anything, bankrupt and with no way for his family to pay but his life insurance. So he said to me, he said, 'Mike, if you've got a thousand dollars in ready cash, you can have the house and I can get clear.' Now it turns out I had exactly that, so I went to the bank and gave it to him and he squared with the bank and I got the house. So I hurried home. You remember Mama and I lived in that brick apartment house then? So I went and got your mama and put her in the car and wouldn't tell her where we were going. We drove right up here, outside, and she said, 'Who are we going to see? Who lives here?' and I said, 'We do!'"

Shirley laughed. That was always the best punchline, her mama finding out they owned a big house in the park, a big white house like she'd always wanted, with green lawns and a big garden and two screened porches. It was true that the big white house was bigger than they needed for three people. It had four bedrooms on three floors, five if you counted the maid's room, though they didn't have help that lived in. Molly came in five days a week and cleaned and did laundry and cooked, but she went home to her own house every night. And Frank did the yard and mowed with the push mower and tended the arbor. And if her parents had a dinner party, there was a girl named Nan who wore a uniform and served at the table. You could get her to come in by pushing a hidden electric button under the carpet in front of the hostess's chair.

Not that Shirley was supposed to touch any of the electric bells. They were for adults. If she bounced up and down on the buttons making them ring, Molly would tell her to behave. Molly told her to behave a lot. She wasn't supposed to run in the house or slide down the curved bannister or get her pastel dresses covered in grass stains. She wasn't supposed to go down in the basement because of the coal dust from the steam boiler that kept the house warm in the winter. When it was hot and the air was bad, she couldn't go to the park or the movies or anything because that was when polio spread everywhere.

"The man who had this house before Bob," her daddy said, "had a little girl who died from polio. She was two years older than you are now, and your room was built for her."

So maybe the big white house was haunted, Shirley thought. Maybe her room was haunted by the girl who had died. But if so, she didn't seem to mind Shirley living in her room. Maybe it was nice. Maybe she liked having another girl live there. Shirley decided the girl's name had been Alice, and sometimes she invited Alice to have a tea party with her and her dolls.

"We could be ghost sisters," she said, and she almost believed Alice was really there.

When she was five, the war started and terrible things were happening to lots of people far away. In the evening her daddy and mama would sit by the radio and listen to reports on bombings and deaths and battles. One time when her daddy took her up to bed, afterward she said she was scared. "Are you going to have to go fight?"

He shook his head. "I'm forty-seven years old, toots. They're not drafting old guys like me. I did my bit in the Great War, and wild horses couldn't get me back to France. No sir. *Dulce et decorum est* and all that, but this boy's no sucker, let me tell you."

Shirley frowned. She didn't understand a bit of that, except that he was too old. "Mama's younger than you."

"That she is. Swept this old dog right off his feet with her beauty. I was on a sales call in this little burg and took one look at Cordelia and pow! Married in three months, and her parents having kittens the whole time. They didn't think she should marry an Irishman from New York City. Now doesn't she have a big house and a car and everything a woman could want?" He tucked her under the covers. He'd go downstairs in a minute to mix Mama a B & B and they'd sit listening to the radio for a while longer. "Don't you worry about anything. You're my princess and nothing bad is ever going to happen to you."

———— • ————

And nothing did. Shirley had piano lessons and she walked to school five blocks away. Her friends lived in the park too, and when the war was over, they all went to the beach together, stayed in beach houses all summer, weren't supposed to talk to sailors, and mostly didn't.

She took art lessons and learned to paint still lifes of flowers. It was fun to try to get the shades right, to try to get the petals to look like they had texture and weight. She tried to explain it to her mother once. "Lilies are like silk, because they look fine and thin but the petals are actually rather thick, like heavy dupioni. Roses are more like chiffon—that's why they can be fragile in the vase.

Camellias shatter, but the petals are sturdy like taffeta, and there is so much color variation in a small area, like watered taffeta."

"Flower arranging is a very genteel hobby," her mother said, but that wasn't the point.

Shirley did cotillion and applied to college. "I want to major in art," she said.

Her father was fine with that. "Whatever major you want, toots. It doesn't really matter. So whatever makes you happy, as long as it's at a girls' school with a good reputation."

"Why do I have to go to a girls' school?" Shirley asked. "There are coed colleges now. Lots of girls are doing it."

"Not nice girls," her mother said, and that ended that. Shirley knew exactly what she was supposed to do. She was supposed to go to a fine women's college and get an MRS Degree. That meant finding someone with a good job and a stable future.

Which of course she did. In the fall of 1956 she met Hank at a sock hop. He was just as prep as she was, with wire-rimmed glasses and slicked back hair. His father owned an insurance agency and he was going to be a partner as soon as he graduated, Henry Jr. right alongside Henry Sr. He wore sport coats and liked watching college football. He didn't know anything about art and literature was just a course he dreaded, not a way to slide away to another world where anything could happen. He was going to make a lot of money, or at least that's what everyone said. She supposed she was in love with him. At least she couldn't think of a reason not to be, so they got engaged.

The summer before her senior year in college, the summer before the summer she was going to marry Hank, in 1957, her daddy took her and her mama to Europe. They traveled on an ocean liner (none of this parvenu airplane stuff!) and visited castles and famous places. Shirley wandered through the Louvre and the Uffizi in kind of a dream, spending hours trying to get a good look at the brushwork of Raphael or the composition of Caravaggio. There was fashion too. Her mother wanted to shop, and if great designers were beyond their means, there were many more modest apostles at the temples of fashion, and one could always look just like one could in a museum.

Two-toned Chanel shoes and fine Burberry coats were works of art too. Her daddy bought her the Hermes scarf she yearned for, silk so fine with colors so clear that it seemed like Tiffany glass turned to water. To live in this world would be incredible.

And maybe that was a plan. Home in the States, back in school, Shirley had an idea. At Christmas break she sprung it on her parents.

"I've been thinking about not marrying Henry," she said at dinner one night.

Her mother put her glass down on the white tablecloth. "What?"

"I think I'm too young to get married."

"You're twenty-one," her mother said.

"Well then." Her father looked at her keenly. "Has Henry misbehaved? Has he pressured you?"

"Um, no." Shirley didn't think a few kisses in the back of a car counted as pressure. They hadn't gone too far, and he hadn't really tried to. They just kind of mutually agreed that sex had to wait for marriage, and there really wasn't any rush. It wasn't like it was so great, Shirley thought. I mean, people made a big deal out of it, but not having sex with Hank wasn't difficult.

"Because if he has, I'll make him wish he was never born," her daddy said.

"Really, it's nothing like that." Shirley fiddled with her heavy linen napkin. "I was just thinking." She took a deep breath. "My friend Eileen has a job in New York. She's going to be working as an editorial assistant at *Town & Country*. And a lot of the fashion magazines hire artists because a bunch of the houses won't let photographers see their collections until the runway shows. And the designers themselves, not just the big ones but the department store designers and buyers, they have artists too! They do everything right down to the ads that run in the papers showing that Sears has a sale on ladies' shoes. Eileen said I could come with her and stay with her and the two girls she's sharing an apartment with and I could find a job in fashion." She stopped, out of words and breathless.

Her father put his fork down again. "Absolutely not. I won't give you permission to do any such thing."

"But why?" Shirley felt tears starting in her eyes. "Daddy, you know me. You know I'll be good and I won't get into any trouble!"

"It's not about whether you'll be good. God knows you're a good girl. But I grew up in New York, and I know what the city is like for a single woman. A working woman! Do you realize you'd be around men all day? It wouldn't be like college. You'd be around men all the time—hard-driving, hard-drinking men who are used to having their own way. Fashion is a madhouse, toots, and so is advertising. They'd love to take a girl like you out, get a couple of drinks into her, and have their way. They'd destroy you. A girl never recovers from something like that."

"But I would never..."

"Have sex?" her mother asked. "Yes, you would, darling. Whether you wanted to or not. And even if you wanted to, premarital sex is a minefield. Disease, pregnancy, degenerate people..."

"Your mother and I have worked our whole lives to keep you safe," her daddy said. "We never want anything to happen to you. Don't you under-stand? One wrong move, one bad party, one fast-talking jerk, and your life is over. You'll never be the same again. You'll never marry, never have children, never have any kind of normal life. You may even go insane and spend the rest of your life on the shrink's couch. All for what? To draw some pictures of clothes? Toots, if you want to draw pictures of clothes, draw all you want. But you are not getting a job in New York. We love you too much to let you destroy your life that way."

Shirley bit her lip. Her hands were shaking under the table. Rage? Fear? What if all that happened to her? Of course they loved her. Of course they wanted what was best. "It was just an idea," she said.

Six months later, on June 17, 1958, Shirley marched down the aisle on her daddy's arm in a gown of white crêpe de chine with Belgian lace to where Hank waited for her in front of the altar. "This is the happiest day of my life," she said, and wondered if she meant it.

Spring Equinox: A Better World

Shirley, born in 1936, is in the middle of the Silent Generation, the generation too young for World War II and too old to be Baby Boomers. Like many children of Lost Generation parents, the generation of World War I rather than World War II, she grew up protected and cherished to a degree that the immediately previous generations couldn't have imagined. Her parents, Mike and Cordelia, had just achieved an upper middle-class lifestyle against all odds. For them, life was a crapshoot, a dangerous gamble that some won and some lost. If you made the wrong moves, your family could collect your life insurance if you killed yourself. If you made the right moves, or were just exceptionally lucky, you'd be the one who bought the house for a song. However, in what they perceived as an increasingly dangerous world, protecting their children meant cocooning them against all possible "bad influences."

Like other girls her age, Shirley was taught that "good girls" make good grades, go to good schools, marry good boys, have good children, and settle down to hostess for their husbands and help their careers. If they were dissatisfied, they did not yet even have the words to describe their malaise, "the problem that has no name." Betty Friedan gave them the vocabulary in 1963 when she wrote *The Feminine Mystique* about women like Shirley—educated women with young children who found themselves extraordinarily unhappy despite their apparently perfect lives. She argued, among other things, that having been protected from pain and the maturation that adversity provides results in arrested development, keeping women emotionally immature and unfulfilled, and that protecting women from potential harm actually did incredible harm in itself. She argued that a fulfilled life derived from being a fulfilled person whose intellectual and sexual needs were met as well as their emotional ones.[21] *The Feminine Mystique* was a hugely influential book and kicked off the second wave of the women's movement.

However, for many women like Shirley, it was too late. Divorced in the 1970s with children, over forty with no work experience, they watched women twenty years younger leap ahead into careers and in many cases

---

21. Betty Friedan, *The Feminine Mystique*, W.W. Norton and Company, New York, 1963

into matrimony with older, successful husbands who now sought fulfillment rather than just responsibility. More than two-thirds of men who divorced remarried, while only about 40% of women ever did throughout the rest of their lives.[22] In terms of career opportunities, only a lucky few managed to reenter the work force and achieve financial stability. Most wound up in low-paying "pink collar" jobs, contributing to an enormous gender gap in income.

Men too had difficulties. Coming of age with no great challenge, with the pressure to conform and prove their manhood by their lack of emotion, Silent men also had a "midlife crisis." Breaking out of conformity into the sexual revolution their juniors led, they pushed back against the institutions their seniors, the Greatest Generation, had built. As Alan Aldas and Carl Sagans, they tried to create a gentler vision of masculinity—only to be mocked for it by their punk rock sons. Too old and too young, the Silent never seemed to find their feet. They remain the only generation in American history to never produce a president, only the losing candidates Walter Mondale, Michael Dukakis, and John McCain.

The Silent Generation paid a steep bill for being the most protected and people-pleasing generation in American history, at least until their grandchildren came along.

Allie's Story

Allie opened her eyes on the world at 6:08 a.m. on June 10, 2002. She let out a long, healthy baby scream, and the nurse-midwife laid her against her mother's breast, her tiny, bloody head under Jessica's chin. Her father, Jason, was crying, and his tears fell on her head, on her flailing arm, as he promised to protect her forever. The world was a scary place, and she had almost never existed at all.

In later years, she heard the story every September. It came with the retrospectives of 9/11, with the pictures of burning and collapsing towers, and she was never sure when that story became her story. Her mother believed

---

22. Gretchen Livingston, "The Demographics of Remarriage," Pew Research Center, November, 2014

she'd died that day and returned nine months later, and maybe it was true and maybe it wasn't, but the part she was sure of was this: Her parents had decided they were ready to have a baby and had stopped using birth control, and then 9/11 happened. They talked about whether to go through with it, whether they could bring a child into this world, and decided that they had to have as much courage as their ancestors and do it anyway. They'd asked the gods to help and did a ritual to offer a new chance at life for someone whose life work had been cut short. Mom had conceived the next week while missing posters still hung hopefully all over New York, graying with ash. Maybe Allie had come from that and maybe not, but either way she knew that her birth was an act of faith. Her parents had given her as a hostage to the future, an act of hope that the world wasn't as chaotic and evil as it seemed.

When she was little, they lived in an apartment in the city. Her dad was a coder for a software company and her mom did tech support for the medical database for the hospital. Then they moved into a nice townhouse in a bedroom community when she was five so that she could go to a good school when she started kindergarten. It was three stories and she had her own room and bathroom way up on the third floor, where she could look out across the roofs of the houses across the street to the lights and the shopping center along the highway beyond. Every house looked just alike, and nobody ever seemed to play on the playground that was just expensive equipment sitting in a big square with fresh-laid turf around it, but school was fun.

Allie was in first grade when Barack Obama was elected president. Her parents talked about how important and good this was, not just because he was the first black president, but because bad things were happening with money and the economy, which didn't make a lot of sense to her, at least until her dad lost his job the next spring. The software company he worked for had been sold to another company, and they were consolidating. Her dad worked from home doing "gig work," which was awesomely cool because he could spend a lot of time with her, and she could go with him to get groceries and do everything after school rather than be in aftercare. They played *Final Fantasy* together and he let her get all the points, even if she didn't realize it at the time. Mom got home really late each night. She was stressed out.

It was a year later that her parents sat down with her after dinner for a big talk. They were moving, not just out of their house but across the country. "Why?" Allie asked. "What about school? What about my soccer team? What about Brownies?"

"We have to do a short sale," her dad said, "to avoid foreclosure."

"What does that mean?"

"It means we owe more money on the townhouse than it's worth," her mom said. "We bought at the top of the market. We're upside down on the mortgage. We owe more money than we have. And Dad doesn't have a full-time job right now. We've got to sell the house before we lose it. It's too expensive to live here, honey," her mom said.

"And your mother has an offer from a university to manage their database, but we have to move where the university is. It's a small town and it's a lot less expensive to live there." Her dad looked harried. "You'll like it. There's a Brownie troop there too."

"Maybe we could take in boarders instead, like Kit?" Allie suggested.

Her mom looked confused, but dad knew exactly which American Girl books she was talking about. "I don't think that's going to work for us," he said. "But you're right. This is like the Great Depression. And we just have to work as hard as Kit and her parents did."

Later, after all the lights were out, Allie slipped down the stairs. Her parents were talking in the kitchen and couldn't see her on the dark stairs.

"You've got to know when to fold them." Her dad put his arm around her mom. "Right now we're just going to lose our shirts. We can't keep avoiding paying your student loan payments. If we don't get out of the mortgage, we're going to have to declare bankruptcy."

"That won't erase student loan debt."

"I know. It's ours until we die."

"Or we pay it off in 2032."

"Right." her dad smiled what might have been a devil-may-care smile. "Presuming we all live that long."

"Presuming that."

Allie crept back upstairs very quietly. She knew what she had to do. She had to be very quiet and helpful and not make any trouble at all.

———— • ————

Their new town was nice. It was scary at first to be in a new school, but Allie was determined to be friendly and outgoing, so she met a lot of kids and her teacher liked her.

When her grandmother came to visit at Christmas, everyone acted like the move was a great thing and nobody said anything about short sales or foreclosures. Her mom whispered to her dad in the kitchen, "Why don't we ask your mom?"

He shrugged. "All she's got is Social Security and whatever she makes from selling her paintings. She owns the beachfront condo she bought with the money my grandfather left her, but the alimony stopped when Dad died. No, everything is fine."

And that was what he said at dinner. Everything is fine. Allie kept up a constant chatter about how fun school was and how fun everything was.

Her grandmother acted like she believed it, at least until dessert. "You wanted to be a movie director, remember that, Jason? You said you were going to win an Oscar. You had all these big plans."

"There are other ways of telling stories besides making movies," her dad said.

"You were going to make a living with video games." Her grandmother shook her head. "I told you that you needed to do something practical. Everyone needs a practical way to make a living."

"I do make a living doing video games."

"Nobody ever won an Oscar for gig work."

It got very quiet for a long moment. "Grandmother, have I shown you my doll collection?" Allie asked. "I really want to show you. They're so special." And she led her grandmo ther to her room to see.

Not too long later, Allie came in after school to find her dad working in his home office, a bunch of drawings and sketches around him that didn't look like the boring stuff he usually did. "What're you doing?"

He looked excited, his hair falling down in his eyes. "I'm working on a secret project."

"Is this a thing that's secret like not talking about being Pagan at school?" Allie sat down on the floor cross-legged and the cat climbed into her lap.

"Well, that would probably be ok in this town, but you never know. No, it's not that kind of secret. Just something that Mom and I and our friend Randy are working on, a way of telling stories. It's creating open-source software for games, so that people can create their own and tell their own stories. Randy and I are writing code, and your mom and I are writing a story."

"What kind of story?" Allie loved Dad's stories.

"A story about brave rebels winning against all odds to overthrow a tyrannical king. About honor and sacrifice and maybe love. Because we need those stories. Do you see? How much do stories mean to you?"

Allie nodded. She did see. She read and read and read because just about any problem that anyone ever had, somebody had solved it in a story, no matter how awful it was.

"Stories teach us how to be better people. They show us how to be happy. And they let us meet all kinds of people we've never met in real life."

"I think that's a good idea," Allie said seriously. "Only I expect it doesn't make any money."

"Not right now, no," he said. "Maybe someday. But the story is the important thing, because being good is more important than being rich."

"Can't you be good and rich at the same time?"

"I'm not sure about that," Jason said. "It doesn't usually work out that way."

Allie nodded, but she wondered if it wouldn't be worth it to be a little less good and a little richer.

Beltane: Spring into Summer

Born in 2002, Allie is the very beginning of the generation now called the Homelanders. Growing up with two wars and economic problems larger than any since the Great Depression, the Homelanders have been protected by their Gen X parents in a complete turnaround from the way Gen X was parented. Things that never caused anyone to blink in 1975, like leaving kids home alone, warranted a call to Child Protective Services in 2015.

At the same time that protectiveness has increased, the world has gotten far more unsafe. For example, in the entire decade of the 1980s, 35 children were killed in shootings at schools nationwide. Between 2005 and 2015, the number increased fourfold to 141. The number of children in foster care continues to increase, reaching nearly half a million by 2016.[23] This is twice the number from 1985.[24] In 1993, the combat deaths of 19 soldiers in Mogadishu, Somalia, prompted the withdrawal of US troops from the zone of conflict.[25] In the first fifteen years of US involvement in Afghanistan, 1,865 servicemembers have been killed in action.[26]

The Homelanders, like the Silent Generation before them, are growing up in a world of growing shadows. The fortunate among them are precariously protected by parents hyperaware of every danger. However, that too has its downsides. Helicopter parents parachute in to make every decision for their children who no longer play outside with unstructured time. Many malls no longer allow teenagers to visit unaccompanied by parents, and young teens in food courts or fast food restaurants without adult supervision are likely to be questioned by security guards. There have been well-publicized cases in recent years where kids playing on public playgrounds without their parents have been taken into CPS custody. There are now even apps that allow parents to track their college students on campus and see if they're going to class.[27] Through various other apps, a parent can follow a child's whereabouts 24/7 through GPS, knowing if they're in their dorm or off campus at a club, walking back from the library late or in the gym for a blameless

23. "Number of Children in Foster Care Continues to Increase," US Department of Health and Human Services, November 30, 2017

24. "Trends in Foster Care," US Department of Health and Human Services, October 8, 1991

25. Mark Bowden, "Black Hawk Down," *The Philadelphia Enquirer*, November 16, 1997

26. US Department of Defense, www.defense.gov, accessed April 6, 2019

27. Class120.com, accessed April 6, 2019

workout.[28] Teens face an enormous amount of structure and scrutiny that would have been just plain bizarre to Generation X.

But is it actually beneficial? As some wonder if the Homelanders don't know who the heroes are and are searching for authentic moral decisions, it's wise to remember the experience of the Silent Generation, who stood in the same place on the wheel. Growth comes from making mistakes and coming of age requires real risks and real danger. And yes, real danger means real harm for some.

If Shirley had gone to New York and lived in the *Mad Men* world as an innocent young single woman, harm might have befallen her. She might have been sexually assaulted or mugged, faced workplace harassment or developed a drinking problem. She might have had an out-of-wedlock baby, a tragedy in the 1950s. She might have entered into an abusive relationship. None of those things happened to her. Instead, she gave up a career she truly wanted, entered into a loveless marriage, never found sexual fulfillment, and harmed her children through her bitterness. It was not until she was in her sixties that she found artistic success.

Will her granddaughter Allie have the same experiences? Or will she have instead the experience of being made stronger by overcoming pain, of being made wiser by encountering danger? Coming of age requires facing actual challenges, both large and small. The Homelanders, like the Silent before them, don't face a lack of role models for heroism but a lack of opportunity. If you never have a choice, how can you make the right one? If you can never make a wrong one, how can you grow?

One of the questions, as we move deep into the Winter, the Crisis era, is whether the Homelanders will be challenged as a generation, and what their response will be. The story of Allie's Beltane is yet to come, a story that will come to fruition in the 2030s. Who will she be then? A mother? An artist? A counselor? All of the above? Or will she be a victim, a cautionary tale, a story on the news illustrated by a social media picture of a radiant young woman

---

28. Randi Olin, "Why I Won't Be GPS Tracking My College Freshman," *The Washington Post*, October 29, 2015

while the reporter solemnly talks about her tragic death? Allie's story does not yet have an ending or even a middle.

Responding to the Winter-Born

For one final time in walking the seasons of the Great Wheel, take out your blank book or notebook for journaling. Turn on the computer if that is what you have been using. And remember, there are no right or wrong answers to these questions. We all understand the world from our own perspective on the Great Wheel.

Shirley's Story

- What is your immediate emotional response to Shirley's story?

- Do you identify with Shirley? With others in her life? How are you similar? How are you different? If you share some of the same experiences but were shaped differently by them, why do you think that was?

- Do you think Shirley has made wise or unwise decisions about her future? Why do you think that?

- What do you think of Shirley's parents, Mike and Cordelia? What do you think of her relationships with them? Why do you think they make the decisions they do? If you were writing Mike's story as part of the Lost Generation, a new story in Summer-born with Jason and Nikia, what would that story be about?

- What do you think of Shirley's love of art and fashion? Is she talented? Or shallow? Why do you think that?

- Knowing that Shirley and Hank will become Jason's parents in the Summer-born chapter, how does knowing Shirley's story alter your viewpoint on them in that chapter? How does it alter your viewpoint on them in Allie's Story?

- Does Shirley remind you of people you knew? What has happened to those people in later years?

If you are Winter-born in the next cycle (born in 2002 or later), consider these questions:

- Have you experienced some of the same social trends or experiences as Shirley even though you live in a different era? How are those experiences the same or different?

- Have you made some of the same decisions as Shirley? What happened to you as a result of those decisions? Have you faced the same decisions but made different choices? What happened as a result of those choices? If you stood before those choices again, what decisions would you make?

If you are not Winter-born, consider these questions:

- If you are old enough to remember some of the trends and social movements of Shirley's life, how did you experience them differently than she does? How was your understanding or perspective different?

- Does Shirley remind you of people you have known, whether elders or juniors? How do you relate to those people?

- How are Shirley's experiences different from yours or those of people you know because of her moment in time?

Allie's Story

- What is your immediate emotional response to Allie's story? Why do you feel that way?

- Do you identify with Allie? With others in her life? How are you similar? How are you different? If you share some of the same experiences but were shaped differently by them, why do you think that was?

- What do you think will happen to Allie next?

- What do you think of what has happened with Jason and Jessica who we met in Summer in Jason's Story? Are you surprised by the trajectory of their lives? Disappointed? Pleased?

- What do you think of Allie's experience of the Great Recession? How might her experience have been different if she had been older? Younger? How does it feel to examine such recent events through the lens of history?

- How do Allie and her grandmother, Shirley, share some of the same experiences? How are they different?

If you are also Winter-born (in 2002 or later), consider these questions:

- Are you older or younger than Allie? Did you experience some of the same events or social trends? How are your memories of those events different from hers? How are they the same?
- Does Allie remind you of people you know?

If you are not Winter-born, consider these questions:

- If you are old enough to remember some of the events and trends of Allie's life, how did you experience them differently than she does? How was your understanding or perspective different?
- Does Allie remind you of people you have known? How do you relate to those people?
- How are Allie's experiences different from yours or those of people you know because of her moment in time? How might your experiences be different if you were older or younger?

····· Chapter 9 ·····

Winter, a Season of Crisis

The Homelanders are Winter-born, children of this current season. Around the year 2020 we are deep in the season of Winter on the Great Wheel. Now it's time to explore this season more thoroughly.

Winter is the Crisis era. Winter is a time that tests all living things. Even in our age of technology, when few people in the United States must brave the elements constantly or live without electricity or artificial heat, winter kills. Icy roads, nor'easters and ice storms, Midwestern blizzards—winter is dangerous and still sometimes fatal. We, who watch the weather, know that winter is not always predictable. It may be impossible to know if a storm will drop only rain on our location or a foot of snow. Will we merely have a soggy day or an ice storm that snarls traffic and brings down power lines? When will winter begin? We can't know, looking ahead from summer, or even from the perspective of a few weeks ahead, if December 15 will be bad or not. We can't know, as we try to plan our lives with calendars and schedules, if January 22 is a good day to have that meeting or if it will have to be cancelled. Often we don't know the day before. Prognostication, even with the aid of advanced modeling and satellites, is only so good.

However, long-range forecasting can identify major trends. A dip in the jet stream means that winter weather will affect more of the continental US. The conjunction of moisture and arctic winds will create a storm. The effects of long-range climate phenomena like El Niño and La Niña are well known. It may not be possible to say in advance what the weather will be on a particular day, but it's possible to make a general prediction: a colder period with more moisture is coming, or the next few weeks promise to be warmer and dryer than average. Likewise, there are things we can infer from our own experience. While it's not 100% certain that a particular day will have good weather, in much of the US it's more likely to be sunny and warm in April than in January! We may not be able to say in advance what day the first winter storm will strike, but we can make generalizations that are usually correct: it won't snow until after Midwinter here, or February is usually the most difficult month. Seasons follow one another in a particular order, and we, like our ancestors before us, can predict the cycle in general terms—harvest moon, blood moon, snow moon, wolf moon—even if that doesn't give us precise forecasts of particular events.

Likewise, the seasons of the saecula are predictable. The full cycle of the great year is about eighty years. Each season is about twenty. Of course, each season of the great year doesn't begin and end precisely on the mark, any more than autumn always begins precisely on September 21. Cool rains may sweep in on September 17, making it feel like fall. Or warm weather may linger into October with no perceptible change in the color of the leaves, with only the lengthening night as a guide that autumn is here. It varies from year to year. Likewise, the seasons of the great year may vary by a few years, coming in at twenty-one years to one season, twenty-three to another, seventeen to a third. However, if you look back about eighty years at any point on the wheel of the saecula, you should find yourself in the same season you now experience, just as if you look back twelve months on the Wheel of the Year, you will find yourself in the same place.

Let's take our previous example of World War II. The war ended in 1945, the climax of a Crisis era that reshaped the world. Eighty years before that, in 1865, the Civil War ended. Eighty-two years before that, in 1783, the Treaty of Paris ended the American Revolution. Eighty-six years before that, the Crisis era ended that had peaked with the Salem Witch Trials and King William's War, dividing the British colonies that would become the United States from those that would become Canada. Each of these moments was the resolution of a long, dark Winter. Each of these moments crystalized a new order that would dominate until the next crisis point. Each of these moments was the turning of the great year, the zero-point beginning and ending of saecula.[29]

In each case, this point was preceded by the season of Winter, by a long Crisis era before it. The world crisis that ended with World War II began in the 1920s, some twenty years before. What date did Winter begin? One could argue that it began in 1929, with Black Friday and the stock market crash that began the Great Depression. Or perhaps it began in 1922, with the rise to power of Mussolini, the first of the major Fascist dictators. Perhaps it was with the election of Herbert Hoover in 1928. A case could be made for each date, but sometime around 1925, Autumn turned imperceptibly into Winter. When did the Civil War crisis begin? Was it with the Compromise of 1850? With Texas joining the United States in 1845, thereby causing the Mexican War? With the debates of Calhoun and Webster from 1840? A good argument could be made for each date, but sometime around 1845 Winter began. Each of these Winters began approximately sixty years after the previous Winter ended.

Year	Crisis Era	Events
1675–1697	Colonial Crisis	King Philip's War, Bacon's Rebellion, Salem Witch Trials
1763–1783	Revolutionary Crisis	Navigation Acts, Stamp Act, American Revolution
1845–1865	Civil War Crisis	Mexican War, Bleeding Kansas, John Brown's raid, Civil War
1922–1945	World War Crisis	Rise of Fascism, Great Depression, World War II
2005?–2025?	Millennial Crisis	Afghanistan and Iraq Wars, Great Recession, Crisis of 2020

---

29. William Strauss and Neil Howe, *Generations: The History of America's Future*, Morrow and Company, New York, NY, 1991

Now let's count forward. If we know that World War II ended in 1945, and thus ended the last Winter, when would the next Winter be? The next Winter would begin around 2005 and end around 2025. When did Winter begin? With the terrorist attacks on September 11, 2001? With the invasion of Iraq in March 2003? With the stock market crash on September 29, 2008? With the election of Barack Obama six weeks later? Future historians can fruitfully debate which event, which storm, was actually the first storm of Winter, but we all know that Winter came. We entered a Crisis era.

We can expect this Crisis era to peak and then resolve sometime around 2025.[30] What will that peak be? War with North Korea? Constitutional crisis? Impeachment? Weather-related disaster caused by climate change? War with Russia or China? Revolution or dissolution? There are many possibilities clamoring for our attention on news websites every day.

Perhaps, like previous crises, it will be a combination of more than one factor. Assuredly, it will be some of the factors currently on the table. After all, while no one in 1938 could have told you that the Japanese would bomb Pearl Harbor on December 7, 1941, General Billy Mitchell had hypothesized exactly such an attack in the early 1930s. Those in the know in military circles were aware of his prediction, whether or not they considered it likely. Also in 1938, it was certainly clear to those who followed current events that the situation in Europe was becoming more and more precarious, with Hitler throwing out the terms of previous treaties and building a war machine. It may not have been possible to predict exactly how and when war would come, but it was a good bet that it would. Likewise, the escalating problems in the 1850s, culminating with John Brown's raid on Harpers Ferry, made it clear that a crisis was approaching, even if the exact shape of the Civil War wasn't apparent. In each case, the storm builds and builds until some event, one of these factors, reaches a tipping point. Something is the straw that breaks the camel's back, the critical event.

The pattern of the saecula, the long-range forecast as it were, suggests that tipping point will be reached between 2018 and 2021, and that the reso-

---

30. William Strauss and Neil Howe, *The Fourth Turning*, Broadway Books, New York, NY, 1997

lution of this crisis will occur around 2025. In other words, we stand at Imbolc on the great year. We are deep in Winter. Terrible storms are behind us, but the worst of Winter's fury is ahead. The Spring Equinox is nearing but we do not know on what date Spring will truly come.

Here is another thing we know: Spring will come. No matter how cold and forbidding the last month or so of winter can be, we know that spring will come. It is inevitable. There are signals in the natural world that tell us it will be so, even when the storm's fury rages. The days are lengthening. Beneath the soil, roots are growing as plants prepare for spring growth. Animals that give birth in the spring are mating or have mated, females heavy with the young who will be born with the sun. Buds swell on the tips of branches. At Midwinter, none of these things were true. The world could simply get darker and darker, colder and colder, sinking into eternal night and frozen oblivion. Now, we can see signs that won't happen. We do not know when it will come, or if we will survive the storms to see it, but spring will come.

Looking back at past eras, this same pattern could be seen. For example, the technologies that would knit the world together over the next saeculum were in infancy in 1938: television, international aviation, the idea of satellites. In 1938 those were nascent, or else the stuff of speculative articles or the pipe dreams of eccentric millionaires, but they were on the horizon. In 1938, the old colonial empires were struggling to maintain their grasp on far-flung territories, challenged by nationalist movements that few predicted would amount to anything. The postwar world map was as yet unimaginable. Or rather, it was imagined, but dismissed as impossible. Everyone knew how things had worked for nearly eighty years. Drastic change would never happen.

The second thing we can know is this: drastic change *will* happen. We may not know yet which of the competing visions of that change will be the one that becomes reality, but we can be certain that one of them will. We will not go back to 1992. The Wheel of the Year does not turn backward. Nor does the Great Wheel. We cannot return to Autumn Equinox from Imbolc. The only way to Midsummer from Imbolc is through Spring Equinox. Clinging to the idea that we can go back to some previous season is pointless. The only way to go is forward. Yes, Midsummer will come again, and so will

Autumn Equinox, but only in the next saeculum, in due course of time. We must accept and embrace the idea of drastic change. We are standing at a moment as profound and important as 1858 or 1938, facing an upheaval that will mark everyone who lives in this time. We must face the crisis with courage and compassion.

Visualizing Crisis

Nuclear apocalypse, zombie apocalypse, climate apocalypse—we have many ways to visualize irrecoverable disaster. The story goes something like this: Something happens—a viral mutation, a madman with his finger on the button, or a CGI-worthy sudden dissolution of the Antarctic ice sheet that plunges thousands of tons of ice into the sea—and then people die. Everyone dies. Survivors of the initial disaster shoot each other for canned goods in destroyed grocery stores. They wander, sick and dying, through poisoned cities. Maybe a few people, by killing everyone else trying to survive who gets in their way, manage to hold on a few weeks or a few months, living on dwindling looted supplies and leaving the weak behind to die. But in the end, they all die. There is no cure for the virus. There is no safety from the spreading nuclear winter. There is no protection from hostile Earth. This is the story of the last days of humanity.

We've all seen this movie or read this book. We know what happens. Ultimately, it doesn't matter what the heroes do. Their actions are futile. All they can do is show us how to die. And we believe it. Lots of us do, in our hearts. Some of us, like Jason, grew up on *The Day After*, the moral of which is that there is no day after.[31] There is no future. There is no winning or even surviving. Many people follow apocalypse dramas today—*The Walking Dead* being a prime example. People do terrible things to one another, violence escalating to horrific levels, as the audience accepts that this is simply necessary in the end of the world. Everybody's armed, and only a fool is merciful. You kill until you die.

While apocalypse dramas have always existed, consider for a moment the impact of apocalypse drama on our society today, especially the zombie nar-

---

31. *The Day After*, directed by Nicolahs Meyer, ABC Circle Films, DVD, 1983

ratives where neighbors are less than human, a ravening horde that must be killed and cannot be reasoned with. Consider for a moment the social impact of even half believing this story. One might believe the monsters are not creatures from outer space or sexy vampires spreading tainted blood, but brown-skinned humans in torn clothes who want to rip apart your children and will if you don't blast them with your assault rifle. And even if you win the encounter, there is no winning in the end. There is no reversing the plague. In the end, everyone will die.

Apocalypse is final. That's inherent in the concept. It's the last crisis, the end of the world. However, there are other ways to examine eras of extreme crisis that are far more useful and true to our current situation than imagined viruses or global nuclear war.

Ekpyrosis

Ekpyrosis is a concept in classical Stoic philosophy that also describes the end of an era. It literally means "destruction by fire" and was thought to be a periodic renewal, like a forest fire. Fire sweeps through the mature forest. Animals that are able to flee run before it while even mighty trees are burned to the ground. The fire burns inexorably until it reaches some natural barrier or rain comes, leaving smoldering ashes behind where there was once a thriving ecosystem. The day after the fire, little remains. Life is extinguished.

Or is it? Roots far beneath the soil survive. Seeds, scattered and lying fallow in green times in the shadow of the great trees, germinate in response to new sunlight. Ants and other burrowing insects dig their way out of their bunkers. The wind brings seeds, too, and birds who eat newly visible insects. Within a few years, a meadow grows where a forest once stood. Grazing animals live there, butterflies flutter from wildflower to wildflower, and small animals tunnel in the soft earth. In a decade young trees are rising, conifers shoulder high. In twenty years there are softwood groves, hardwood saplings coming up, berry bushes that provide food to even more diverse animals and birds. In eighty years a mature hardwood forest stands again as though nothing had ever happened.[32]

Ekpyrosis is the rejuvenation of the world by fire. The world ends and then begins again. The Stoics held that societies were no different than the rest of nature—that in their time each would be consumed and from the ashes would spring up a new society.[33] This cycle was also called a great year, a time lasting according to different philosophers from twenty-six thousand years to about a century, the length of a saeculum. In its time, each society would undergo ekpyrosis and then palingenesis, rebirth in its new form. The seeds of the old society would begin the new.

By studying history, we see this pattern clearly. Kingdoms rise, expand, dominate, and fall. Philosophies emerge, are widely adopted, are transformed, are corrupted, and then fall into disfavor. Empires expand their territories, then overreach and collapse. Sometimes this process takes hundreds of years. Sometimes it takes a decade. But this is the pattern: rise, expansion, overreach, collapse. And then the cycle begins again.

This is not apocalypse. When the Roman Empire collapsed, everyone in Italy didn't die. Tens of thousands were killed in wars and barbarian invasions, but the descendants of the Romans live there to this day. When the Black Death decimated Europe, millions died. And Europe is still there. Descendants of those who survived the plague are reading these words. Measles and smallpox destroyed Native American civilizations—but not Native Americans. Native peoples are not a lost people from the past but a story ongoing today. Even modern wars, with their intensely powerful weapons, do not destroy civilizations utterly. They transform, yes, but every single people who were combatants in World War II still exist. Ekpyrosis, the Stoic concept, fits the way the world actually works far better than the concept of apocalypse.

If indeed we have reached the time for ekpyrosis in the United States, what does that tell us about the future? First, that we are in for a rough ride.

---

32. Debbie Arrington, "Wildfires, Wildflowers Are Part of California's Cycle of Life," *The Sacramento Bee*, Sacramento, CA, July 29, 2016

33. Thomas Rosenmeyer, "Senecan Drama and Stoic Cosmology," University of California Press, 1989

Second, that we will survive. Most of us will come out on the other side of the event into the new world that follows. Third, that the seeds we spread today will determine what the new growth will be.

Stages of Ekpyrosis and the Saeculum

Like winter itself, ekpyrosis has three stages. Let's examine them chronologically. The gathering storm is early winter, when it's obvious that the cold has truly arrived. Days are shorter, nights are longer, the temperature is colder, and we know for certain that it is winter. However, despite these ominous signs, major storms have not yet arrived. We may see a snow flurry or wake up one morning to biting cold that transforms with sunrise and warms as the day continues. It may be gray and rainy but not quite cold enough to ice the streets. We know from our experience of past winters that it's only a matter of time before a storm comes, even if we don't know exactly when. Now is the time to prepare as much as possible, to go to the grocery store while you still can, to buy that ice melt and to get out heavy clothes and blankets.

In the Great Wheel, this is the point where a crisis is apparent. Major problems have been identified and a downward spiral seems inevitable. Saying that something is going to happen has stopped being the alarmist position. Most people can see that things are not normal and that no easy solution presents itself. Looking back at the last cycle, this is where we stood in 1938/39. Was World War II inevitable? Historians can debate whether or not it could have been prevented at some point, but by 1938 the critical decisions were made. There was going to be a war. It was going to be bad. Exactly what day it began and under what conditions was yet to be determined, but in 1938/39 it could not be stopped. We stand in the same place in the cycle eighty years later.

The second stage is the storm itself. It's happening. It's going on right now. All you can do is the work put before you. You cope, day to day, with winter as it roars around you. Conditions are changing rapidly, and surviving means keeping up. You live according to your principles each day.

In the last cycle, this is where we were in 1942–1944. Bombs, rationing, occupied countries, building war machines, serving on the front lines, or simply trying to survive, each person just had to do the thing they were doing. Some had incredibly difficult conditions. Others were lucky not to. But either way, the only thing to do at the time of action is to do what you can to the best of your ability. Some will succeed. Others won't.

The last stage is the waning storm. There is a moment, even in the harshest storm, when you realize it's going to be over. The wind is lessening. The snow is letting up. The cold is less intense. The sun has come out and the snow is melting. It will refreeze tonight, but tomorrow it will melt again. It's possible to imagine that spring will come, or at least that winter will cease. "It might be possible to get through this," people whisper.

This is where we stood in 1945. Winners and losers, living and dead, the war was going to end. It was possible to imagine that in a few months, in a year, this would be over. What would the world look like afterward? Where would national boundaries be? What kind of government would countries have? Which side of a line would you be on? Would those you loved come home? Would you come home? What would the peace look like?

What happens the day after the forest fire? What do you do in the charred woods? How do you get from that day to the day ten years later when young trees are growing? How do you get from 1945 to 1950?

We will face all these questions again. If, indeed, we are dancing the Great Wheel as we have danced before, here is a rough sketch of what we can expect, a long-range forecast as it were, based on our experience with previous Winters.

2016–2019: The gathering storm, the deepening crisis in which it becomes obvious that major events are coming and last preparations are completed.

2020–2024: The storm breaks. Events come to a head. War, civil unrest, international crises, economic disruptions. Old institutions are destroyed or become irrelevant.

2025–2027: The storm begins to blow itself out. Some win and some lose. Resolutions are apparent. New constellations of power are nascent.

2027–early 2030s: The storm passes and Spring comes. Conditions improve for many. The new order solidifies.

The point is not to frighten. The point is to empower. If we know what is going to happen, or even the rough shape of the Winter to come, we can prepare. Not only can we prepare for Winter, but for the Spring to come. This is the point in the saeculum where lasting change happens. We guide that change. The seeds that sprout in the aftermath are the ones we sowed. The ideas that survive, thrive, and guide the new world are the ones we nurture, just as the people who survive and thrive are the ones we nurture. No, we can't guarantee that any particular seed will succeed in the world to come, but we can be 100% certain that the seeds we never plant won't grow into forest giants. We cannot assure success, only failure.

Generations in Crisis

As we explored early in this book with the example of World War II, a person's experience of a Crisis era is defined by their position on the Wheel of Life at the time it happens and the conjunction of their personal wheel with that of the Great Wheel. According to scholars William Strauss and Neil Howe, Crisis eras arrive when the generations are in the same constellation each time. Indeed, Crisis eras arrive *because* the generational constellation reaches a certain configuration, with polarized Spring-born leaders squaring off, the disaffected Summer-born in midlife, and young Autumn-born foot soldiers ready to fight for their side.

Spring-born generations, like Baby Boomers Valerie and Linda, encounter Crisis eras when they are elders. In 2020 the Baby Boomers will be between sixty and seventy-seven. They will comprise the majority of elected officials, judges, others involved with the courts, and the highest military and diplomatic leadership. From Donald Trump to Joe Biden, Nancy Pelosi to John Roberts, Robert Muller to Sonia Sotomayor, Baby Boomers hold the key roles going into the crisis. They are the ones who will shape what form the crisis takes.

Summer-born generations, like Gen Xers Jason and Nikia, encounter Crisis eras in midlife. In 2020 the Summer-born will be between forty and fifty-nine. They will compose the majority of parents, bosses, military officers, and community decision-makers. Some of them will begin the Crisis era relatively unknown and then burst to prominence because of their actions during the crisis. Cory Booker, Tammy Duckworth, Paul Ryan, and many others may not have national name recognition now but will as the crisis intensifies. Still others are little known today outside their field but will be household names over the next twenty years, as Dwight D. Eisenhower, George Marshall, and Earl Warren became in the last cycle. It is the Summer-born who make the decisions that resolve the crisis.

Autumn-born generations like Daniel and Charles encounter Crisis eras as young adults. In 2020 the Autumn-born will be between eighteen, most likely, and thirty-nine. (Exactly when the low end boundary is will depend on when precisely the crisis occurs—the boundary is between those too young to experience it as adults and those who do.) They are the generation of young heroes who will be the major participants in the crisis. They are also the generation who will reshape the world at the end of the Crisis era. We do not know their names now, for only a few have already achieved prominence, but we will if we live to see the world they build. If the pattern holds true, theirs will be the dominant voice in the United States well into the 2060s.

Winter-born generations like Allie and Shirley encounter Crisis eras as children or as very elderly senior citizens. The previous Winter-born generation will be seventy-nine and older in 2020. The current Winter-born will be seventeen and younger, including children still being born. Their participation in the crisis is limited by the accident of their birth. Their role is to refine and make fairer and more beautiful the institutions that the Autumn-born introduce.[34] Their era of power and prominence is yet to come as they steer the course of the next Summer.

How will you experience the crisis? How will you rise to the occasion, as countless millions have in their respective times?

---

34. William Strauss and Neil Howe, *The Fourth Turning*, Broadway Books, New York, NY, 1998

Generation	Imbolc: The Crisis Climax	Age at Imbolc	Role	Examples of Prominent Members
Missionary	World War II	57–81	setting the agenda	FDR, John L. Lewis, George Marshall
Lost	World War II	37–56	active leadership	Dwight D. Eisenhower, Earl Warren, Robert Oppenheimer, Amelia Earhart
Greatest	World War II	16–36	main actors	JFK, Thurgood Marshall, Betty Friedan, Chuck Yeager, Katharine Graham
Silent	World War II, Millennial Crisis	0–15, 78–94	very young or very old	Martin Luther King Jr., Gloria Steinem, Carl Sagan, Ruth Bader Ginsburg
Baby Boom	Millennial Crisis	60–77	setting the agenda	Donald Trump, Hillary Clinton, Clarence Thomas, Bill Gates, Sonia Sotomayor, Steve Bannon
Generation X	Millennial Crisis	40–59	active leadership	Barack Obama, Kamala Harris, Beto O'Rourke, H. R. McMaster, Elon Musk, Tammy Duckworth
Millennial	Millennial Crisis	18–39?	main actors	Mark Zuckerberg, Alexandria Ocasio-Cortez, Nate Silver
Homelander	Millennial Crisis	17 and under?	mostly too young for an active role	Yet to be determined

Aligning the Wheels—Find Your Part in the Story

Your part in the story is defined by the conjunction of your place on the Wheel of Life and your personal choices at the point when Winter becomes severe. We all have different talents and different callings, but even if two people are both called to be healers and serve as medical personnel, their potential choices and opportunities will be different depending on when they were born.

When Imbolc arrives, the climax of Winter and its moment of crisis, each generation has a different part to play in the season. For example, Fred is a Baby Boomer, sixty-eight years old, in the classical quadrant of senectia. He was intending to retire from his medical practice as a general practitioner when the crisis arrived. Instead of retiring, he volunteers with a nonprofit that provides medical care to refugees, taking on the job of helping families and individuals displaced by the crisis. Meanwhile, Antonia is a Gen Xer, and at forty-seven, has just gotten a prestigious teaching position at a hospital. She is in the classical quadrant of virilitas. Her skills are used to deal with the long-term, severe injuries that require multiple surgeries and months of hospitalization, trying to help people not just live but survive and get their lives back. Michaux is twenty-six and is in the classical quadrant of iuventus. He has just begun his residency at the same hospital. However, it rapidly becomes clear that he is needed at a front-line temporary trauma center, immediately saving lives rather than working through the long months of healing afterward. Meanwhile, Charlotte is five, in the classical quadrant of pueritia. She's playing doctor at her grandmother's house, pretending to help because she is too young for any other role. Even if all four people have the same calling—to be a doctor—that calling must be expressed in different ways because of their age.

The chart on page 131 shows the different generations and their roles in the World War II crisis and the coming crisis of 2020, this saeculum's Imbolc, with some examples of prominent members of those generations. Remember, we are specifically talking about a generation's role in the Crisis era, in the season of Imbolc, not their lifetime achievements. For example, Martin Luther King Jr. was too young to participate in World War II because he was only twelve years old when the US entered the war and sixteen years old when the war ended. His life work belongs to the Awakening era, Summer, at the opposite pole of the Great Wheel from Winter. The Winter-born are rarely major actors in Winter, being too young in their first Winter and too old in their second, just as Summer-born are rarely major actors in Summer.

Where do you fit on this table? What does it suggest about what your role is likely to be? How do you think you will fill that role? (Also, remember the boundary between Millennial and Homelander isn't yet clear. It depends on the exact timing of the crisis, because the boundary will eventually be between those too young to take an active role and those who do. It's likely that the current hypothesized boundary of 2001–2002 will actually adjust later and be more like 2004–2005 when all is said and done.)

The Conjunction of Your Wheel and the Great Wheel

The following exercise will help you align your personal Wheel of Life to the Great Wheel of the saeculum. Its purpose is to help you orient yourself to the wheel, beginning in the past and moving into the next few decades. You will once again need your journaling materials, whether you are using a paper journal or electronic journaling. Alternately, you may wish to draw this figure and illustrate or write in it as you work your way around the wheel.

This figure shows the wheel of the great year in its immediate past, present, and immediate future configuration.

If you were born before 1965, begin at the southern node, marked 1965. (If not, move to the next set of questions.) In 1965 the Lost Generation were in old age ranging from 61–80, the Greatest Generation in midlife from 41–60, the Silent in adulthood from 23–40, the Baby Boomers in youth from 5–22, and the new babies being born, ages 4 and younger, were Gen X.

- Who were you in 1965?
- What was your role as Summer began?
- How did you fit into the generational map—how did you relate to the generations older and younger than yourself?

Jot down your answers or illustrate them in the figure you've drawn.

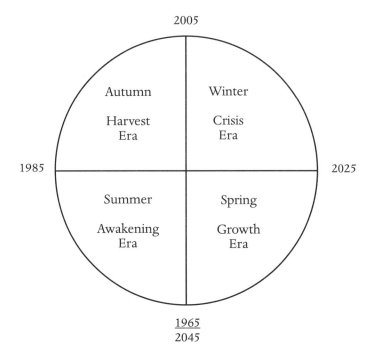

If you were born before 1985, move to or begin at the western node, marked 1985. Around this time, Summer gave way to Autumn, an era of harvests but also of increasing complexity. This is the point where postbellum became antebellum, where the last crisis and the next crisis became equidistant. In 1985 the last Lost Generation survivors were very elderly, the youngest 81. The Greatest Generation were 61–80 and dominated public life. The Silent were in midlife from 43–60. The Baby Boomers had become yuppies instead of hippies and were 25–42. Gen X were children 5–24. Millennials were the new babies on board, 4 years old and younger.

- Who were you in 1985?
- What was your role as Summer ended?
- How did you fit into the generational map—how did you relate to the generations older and younger than yourself?

Write down your answers or illustrate them in the figure you've drawn.

Now let's move ahead to 2005, more or less the beginning of Winter. This is around the time that our current Crisis era began, what Strauss and Howe term the Fourth Turning.[35] The Greatest Generation had begun to disappear from the scene, with the youngest ones 81. The Silent were now in elderhood, ages 63–80. The Baby Boomers were in midlife at 45–62. Gen X now were adults, ages 25–44. Millennials were children and teens 24–4. The very youngest, the newest babies, were the Homelanders, age 3 and younger.

- Who were you in 2005?
- What was your role as Winter began? How did you experience the beginning of Winter?
- How did you fit into the generational map—how did you relate to the generations older and younger than yourself?

Jot down your answers or illustrate them in the figure you've drawn.

Now we will step into the future to 2025, the easternmost node on the chart. This is the point where we can expect the peak and resolution of the crisis, the end of Winter. In 2025 the Silent generation will be 83–plus. The Baby Boomers will be 65–82. Gen X will be in midlife, ages 45–64. The Millennials will now be the young adults 24–44. The Homelanders will be the majority of children and teens, approximately ages 3–23. And there will be the new generation approximately 2 and younger, the next Spring-born generation, whatever they will be called.

- Who are you in 2025?
- What is your role as Winter ends?
- How did you experience the events of the crisis and what part did you play?
- How do you fit into the generational map—how do you relate to the generations older and younger than yourself?

---

35. William Strauss and Neil Howe, *The Fourth Turning*, Broadway Books, New York, NY, 1997

Hero's Tale

Hero stories contain people of all ages, from the wise old sage who provides secret learning to the plucky teenager who rises to the occasion. Hero stories contain people of all archetypes—science fiction shows in particular do a good job of demonstrating how success requires a balanced team. There's the action hero and the techie, the healer and the wheeler-dealer, the diplomat and the scientist, the martial artist and the archaeologist. Science fiction series like *Stargate* and *Star Trek* provide examples of all of these roles and how they work together to save the world.

Think about what role you would fill on a team to save the world. With your journal, or other writing or drawing material, consider your responses to the following questions:

- What skills do you have at a professional level? Are you a doctor, teacher, psychologist, scientist, social worker, or some other profession? If so, how you use those skills in the crisis is most likely your key role.

- Do you already work in a strategically important industry? Are you an electrical company worker, a civil engineer, a soldier, sailor or airman, someone who works in news or broadcasting, someone who works in flood control, firefighting, or air traffic control? If so, doing exactly what you are doing is going to be critical.

- Do you have skills that are not part of your profession (or that you have retired from) which are nonetheless vital? Are you a licensed foster parent, have emergency medical certifications, or simply have great computer skills or people skills? Are you good at advocacy? Caretaking? Coding? Whatever shape the crisis takes, your skills will be needed.

- What can you bring to the table as a Neopagan? Can you use your ritual practice to bring strength and comfort to others who are dealing with difficult times? Are you part of a circle or network that could work together to help people in your community? The role of the priest or priestess can be a vital one in helping communities face crises.

If you feel that you do not have critical skills, or you want to improve some of them, by all means do so. There are, for example, emergency medical classes at most community colleges. Getting a foster care license is about six months of training with one class a week. Becoming involved with the Red Cross or other emergency intervention nonprofits is not time-consuming and gives back to the community in many ways. However, do bear in mind that time is short. If the pattern of this crisis follows previous saecula, you should aim to finish your preparation by mid- to late-2020. This is not the time to hone your skills by starting a master's degree!

The story of the great year is your story. What part you will play is a complex interaction of your personal wheel with the wheel of the saeculum. As we move into the height of the Crisis era, it's time to examine a little more closely what we can expect from Winter.

····· Chapter 10 ·····

Before the Storm

When moviemakers are beginning the process of creating a film, there is a step called previsualization. This is a collaboration between the director, the producer, the writers, and the art departments, including set, costumes, and special effects. The purpose of previsualization is to decide on an overall "look" for the film and to walk through key scenes, imagining how they will appear on film and making adjustments before expensive design components are made and expensive actors are on set. Action scenes are storyboarded, sketches and paintings are made of important moments, and even camera work is imagined. This assures that everyone is on the same page in terms of the production, and that consistent choices are made throughout. That which is not imagined can't be made manifest.

However, we are not in the habit of doing this in real life. We don't look at it the same way a producer with a multimillion-dollar budget does, focused on what will come out three years down the road when this film opens. Often we assume that either everything will be just like it is now, or that we have no control over what happens, and therefore it's pointless to try to direct the tides. And yet previsualization can aid us immeasurably. After all, that which is not imagined can't be made manifest.

Lucas's Story

In June 2030 Lucas graduated from high school. He marched in with his class proudly, only turning his head a little to see if he could spot his family in the giant, echoing basketball arena. He couldn't, but he knew they were there. He knew everyone was there to watch him graduate, his mom and dad; his sister, Destiny; and even his grandma Valerie. They were there somewhere in the seats with phones flashing, Destiny ready to scream his name when he walked across the stage.

Born in 2012, Lucas started school in the era of active shooter drills, when more kids died in classrooms than soldiers overseas. That was what his parents said, and they knew. His mom, Nikia, and his dad, Brandon, had met in Afghanistan when they were both in the army. His mom had been a translator embedded with a rifle company because they needed women who could talk to women in the villages they were in, women who could search houses with women in them, women who could actually get information. His mother, slight, strong, brown-skinned, and fluent in Pashtun thanks to the army, was really good at talking to people. His dad had gone to West Point, and he thought so too. They hadn't had a romance before his mom got wounded, but his dad found her on Facebook after, and when they finally managed to get together a year later, his mom said it was like they'd never been apart. "We were always meant to be," she said.

Destiny loved that story as much as he did. "And that's why my name is Destiny," she said. Mom would hug her and tell her it was true.

"And I'm Lucas," he said. "After the bravest man you knew."

"That's also true," Dad would say. "And someday we'll tell you the story." Their eyes would meet over his head, sad and proud at once. Maybe now that he was eighteen, now that he was graduating from high school, he was old enough for the story.

It was probably a sad story. There were a lot of sad stories that he and Destiny didn't know. He didn't know what had happened during the military action, though he'd been nine years old when his dad had been sent to Texas, and almost ten when he and Destiny had gone to live with Grandma Valerie.

He knew there was bad stuff, and it was why his dad wasn't in the army anymore. "Orders are not a defense against war crimes," his dad said. "That's long established. If you're not going there, you have to resign." Maybe someday he'd know what his dad had been ordered to do, what was too far after Afghanistan. Or maybe he'd never tell him.

He and Destiny had been safe with Grandma Valerie. There had been some scary times when the power was off for days and she and Grandpa Leroy had to figure out how to cook and stuff, but they'd been ok. Not like the kids Grandma Valerie kept getting through her job. She had "un-retired" because there were so many kids in need and she was a social worker. "The United States hasn't had an internal refugee crisis in a hundred years," she said. "We have to step up. Now is the time to be a hero." And at seventy-something, she was.

But she was ok. She was eighty-two now, and Grandpa Leroy died last year, but she was still going strong. Even though she'd never made any money as a social worker, and Grandpa Leroy never made any as a high school teacher, she still had social security and the new guaranteed minimum income, which was good because both their 401(k)s had been wiped out. She still had her little brick house, "thank God it was paid for." And Lucas's mom was looking after her.

Mom was running for the newly reformed House of Representatives this year, one of eight hundred seats representing thirty-seven states. At fifty-two, she was regarded as a rising star. She had a really beautiful web presence on TalkUSA, the national personal media space, with a shifting montage of pictures of her in Afghanistan, her with Lucas and Destiny, in the Deluge, and testifying before the grand jury—under all of which read her motto, "Integrity, Security, and the Dignity of Every Person." Lucas was proud of the motto. He'd made it up, and his mom said it was perfect.

Lucas and the other graduates stood in front of their chairs, then turned and sat down. It was time for all the speeches and awards, and then they'd get their diplomas. He was going to make his parents proud of him. He had to. He had a lot to live up to. But that was ok, because it was just going to get better from here. He was going to study biology and then go to grad school and be a scientist. It was like the president said, "Our grandparents went to the moon. It is our destiny to save the Earth." Lucas was going to answer that call, and one day he'd be a hero too.

Spring Equinox: The First Days of Spring

Lucas's story is an example of previsualization—what does the world look like in 2030 if it's not a dystopia? What would mainly positive outcomes to the crisis look like? If Lucas's story was the next chapter in his family's saga, following his great-grandfather Charles, his grandmother Valerie, and his mother, Nikia, what would that look like? Let's approach his story the same way we approached the others.

Lucas is Winter-born, about the middle of the generation we are now calling the Homelanders. If his life follows the pattern of the saeculum, his childhood will be one of deepening shadows and crisis while adults strive to protect him. The height of the crisis will occur while he is still too young to participate as an adult. His possible roles are victim or protected treasure. His parents, late-born Gen Xers on the cusp of Millennials, are leaders, strong and able decision makers in the crisis. His grandmother Valerie occupies the position of elder and has "un-retired" to provide additional expertise during the crisis, much as the Lost and Missionary Generation air raid wardens and Red Cross workers did in World War II.

Responding to Lucas's Story

- What is your immediate emotional response to Lucas's story? Why do you think you feel that way?
- What do you think of how Lucas's family has developed? Are you surprised by what has happened to Valerie and Nikia? Pleased? Disappointed?
- What do you think will happen to Lucas next? How will the rest of his life turn out?
- What do you think Charles would say if he could know what has happened? What advice do you think he would give Nikia? What advice would he give Lucas?

- What are some things that have changed in the United States in 2030? What do you think of those changes? For example, some of them might be positive: Nikia running for Congress as an African American woman veteran would have been inconceivable to her grandfather. Others might not be positive: Valerie and Leroy lost all their savings. Others might be negative or positive: having eight hundred representatives from thirty-seven states, for example.
- What do you think has happened between 2020 and 2030? What shape can you imagine that the crisis took?
- Do you think this previsualization is likely or not? Is this an outcome you would be satisfied with or not? Why?

Of course Lucas's story is hypothetical. The events and outcomes of the Crisis era are still to be seen. However, as we see the clouds gather on the horizon, it's wise to consider what outcomes we want. In your ideal world, what would things look like in 2030? Given that "nothing happens at all" is not a possibility, what would you like the results to be?

2030: Spring Equinox

For this next exercise, you will once again need your notebook or other journaling materials and the following chart. You may wish to copy it or enlarge it in some way, or you can simply use it as a guide while you journal.

Generation	Age	Activity
Silent	88+	Leaving a legacy
Baby Boom	70–87	Keepers of wisdom
Generation X	50–69	Holding power
Millennials	29–49	Taking responsibility
Homelanders	8–28	Growing and becoming
New Spring-Born	7 and younger	Entering the world

Now think about people you know and love. Sort them into their generation and the life stage they will occupy in 2030. Focusing on positive outcomes, imagine what they will be like in 2030, what they will be doing, and how they will have changed from the present moment.

Returning to the example of Lucas, in 2020 Lucas is in second grade. He lives with his parents. His father is active-duty army while his mother is no longer in service after being wounded in Afghanistan and is now a translator for NGOs working with Pashtun-speaking populations. He has a little sister, Destiny, who is four years old.

In 2030 Lucas is graduating from high school. The time period we are considering is the distance between one child's second grade year and his high school graduation. That's a very manageable amount of time. It's a predictable amount of change—the time it takes one boy to grow up.

In order to reach a destination, we must know where we want to go. Now imagine a happy event that might happen in 2030. Perhaps it's also a graduation. Perhaps it's the birth of a grandchild, the wedding of a loved one, a retirement party or anniversary party, or the celebration of some professional or artistic success. Imagine that you are attending.

- Who is with you? Who is being celebrated and what have they done? Who are they at this point in their life? Who are you?
- Who do you think might be added to your gathering of loved ones between now and then, new children, new in-laws, new lovers? Who do you think might be missed?
- What do you think might have changed in your community in the intervening years? Is this held in a new place or have old places changed? Remember to focus on positive outcomes. We are not creating a dystopian vision—there are plenty of those available. We are previsualizing a non-dystopian future. How do you think this gathering might be better than a similar one today?

Now consider the path between here and there. For example, if you visualize your daughter graduating from college in 2030, what steps must she and the rest of your family take to make that reality? Another example might be that you visualize yourself winning a prestigious professional award in 2030. What do you need to do in your career to achieve that? If you visualize yourself marrying in 2030, what do you need to do to meet the person that you see yourself with then and to become the person who will brim with love on that day?

Farseeing Apollo: A Ritual for Visualizing the Spring Equinox

Like ancient peoples before us, we will invoke farseeing Apollo to help us imagine what we want to come to pass. Apollo is the Greco-Roman god who presides over civilization. Unlike many young male gods who are gods of war or wild places, Apollo rules over reason, over the arts and sciences, over towns, learning, and good governance. He is a patron of medicine and music. However, his older and darker nature is reflected in his aspect as Pythian Apollo, whose oracle at Delphi was one of the great oracles of the ancient world. It's therefore appropriate to call on this god to help us imagine what the future may hold.

As Apollo is also the musician, we will use his medium, music, to transport us on our own journeys to 2030. You will need:

- a means of playing recorded music
- a means of writing
- a white candle
- a quiet place
- incense (optional)

If you are able to light incense, it would be appropriate as incense was a typical offering to Apollo. Bay/laurel is recommended, though pine, fir, balsam, or any woody resin is also appropriate.

First, choose a recorded song that means something to you. It can be instrumental or vocal, classical or rock, hip hop, folk, heavy metal, or whatever you prefer. It should be a song you like and one that you associate with yourself, not a song that you primarily associate with another person or a certain relationship. In other words, "my song" not "our song." It should also be a reasonable length, three to five minutes, not half an hour. Arrange a means of playing it when you reach that point.

Sit in a quiet place and light the candle and incense if you choose to use it.

Say: "Farseeing Apollo, friend of the Muses, averter of evil, help me to imagine my future. Help me to have clarity and insight, born on the wings of music."

Play the music. As you listen, close your eyes. You are listening to this song not now, today, but in June 2030. You have stepped forward a small step in time, a decade or so in your own life, and there you are still listening to this song. You are still you, and this is your music, but it is now 2030.

- How old are you? What milestones do you expect to have reached in your life? Have you graduated from school, changed jobs or professions, changed where you live?

- Imagine the place you live. What is it like? If it is the same place you live now, what changes have you made to it in the intervening time? Who lives there with you, if anyone? Humans? Pets?

- Who are the most important people in your life? Has that changed in the intervening years? Do you have new relationships with partners, children, or grandchildren? Are there people who have left your life in this time? How have the people who are important to you changed? For example, if you now have a twelve-year-old son, how old will he be in 2030 and what do you imagine he will be like? Have your relationships with others changed? For example, if you are now a teen who lives at home with your parents, how do you imagine your relationship with them has changed by 2030, when you are an adult?

- Imagine what's happened to you in the intervening time. Have you had successes or failures? Some of each? Are there challenges you expect to face in the decade or so, and how have you faced them? For example, if you live in a coastal city on the East Coast or Gulf of Mexico, it is likely that you have experienced a hurricane by 2030. If you live in the West in a fire-prone area, it is likely you have experienced a fire. What do you think has happened, both to you and your community?

When the song ends, open your eyes and write down your impressions of what 2030 is to you. You can write it in the same form as Lucas's story, or just jot down some thoughts. The important thing is that you clearly hold in mind what 2030 would look like for you if it were neither apocalyptic dystopia nor everything being exactly the same as it is now.

When you have finished, thank Apollo for his help. Say: "Farseeing Apollo, thank you for the gift of vision." Put out the incense and the candle.

Then look over your work. How do you feel about it? Excited? Disheartened? Worried? Fulfilled?

What are the paths that lead you from here to there? Are there parts of the journey that you can't imagine? For example, if you want to live in Manhattan in 2030 but can't see how you would be able to do that, is that a problem? Do parts of it feel out of your control, like wanting to be married to someone you have not yet met?

What do you want to change about the future you imagine? What do you want to make manifest? For example, if you see yourself in a certain job, what steps can you take to get there? If you see yourself as a parent but don't currently have children, what steps can you take to become a parent?

If you imagined that you have faced significant challenges outside of your control, like hurricanes or wildfires, what can you do to better prepare for them? For example, if you know that it is statistically likely that the place where you live will see a strong hurricane in the next ten years, can you move to higher ground? Can you live in a home that is better built to withstand hurricanes? Can you prepare an evacuation plan and keep it up to date? Farseeing Apollo helps us imagine problems long before they occur so that we can address them when we have time and space, rather than when the crisis is imminent.

There are dark days of Winter between now and that Spring day, but the vision of that Spring day is what will sustain us through the season of crisis.

····· Chapter 11 ·····

Imbolc, a Time for Heroes

When the world is darkest and all hope seems lost, that is when the hero appears. There is a reason that this is the shape of stories told for thousands of years all over the world: it's true. The worst times can bring out the best in us. The hardest tests can inspire acts that are told and retold for generations, stories of fortitude, courage, and grit. We have not chosen to live in this time, but all we can do is our best. For many of us, that best will be extraordinary indeed.

Taz's Story

"Medic! Can I get a medic over here?"

Taz heard the yell through the blowing dust. He got to a crouch, moving forward over the broken glass into the blown-out front of the convenience store. Sweat ran down his face, stinging his eyes, but it was only sweat, not tear gas.

A man with a red cross on his sleeve was down behind the counter, a scatter of dollar bills and gum packets around him as he held a tourniquet on an old guy's femoral artery. He saw Taz's uniform and nodded sharply. "Get your hands in here," he said. "I need to get this on and I can't hold the tourniquet at the same time."

"Ok," Taz said and went to work. This was what he'd trained for. And emotion had never gotten in his way, not since he was old enough to understand it.

———— • ————

The first time Taz heard the phrase "rehoming," he was four years old. Or she was. Everyone said that Taz was a girl named Tamara, but Taz knew better. But he didn't know what rehoming meant, not yet. "I think we need to look into rehoming," his mother said, tearfully, into her phone. "This isn't the child we thought we were getting."

A few days later a lady showed up at their house and said that Taz was coming with her to something called a temporary placement. His mother had a suitcase and two bags, and Taz put his LeapPad and Penguino the stuffed penguin in his backpack, and he went with the lady. He didn't know he'd never come back. Temporary meant he'd be back soon, right?

He stayed with a nice old couple for a little while, but when he asked about going home, they gave weird looks. After a while the old man, whose name was Mike, sat down on the floor with him and explained that he wasn't going back. His mother and father weren't his real mother and father. They were people who had adopted him a couple of years ago, before he was old enough to remember, and now they had decided he wasn't a good fit for their family. He was going to be rehomed, which meant going to some other family.

Taz sat there very still with a toy firetruck in his hand. The entire world was cold. He was cold. They weren't his real family and he was never going home. Finally he said, "Why?"

"It's complicated," Mike said.

Taz screamed. He screamed like a fire engine himself, a loud siren scream, and then he just kept screaming as he hit Mike in the face with the fire engine, pounding and pounding while Mike tried to get up, while his glasses broke and blood ran down his face, screaming until somebody pulled him off.

He was in another house that night, with a dad named Stanley who looked like a wrestler on TV and who said he could handle him. A bunch of his stuff had been left, but he had Penguino, and he went to sleep in a strange bed in a flowered nightgown that they said he had to wear.

He stayed there a little while—long enough for it to be winter—and then it was a therapeutic foster home where there was a nice lady who made everyone eat vegetables all the time and who asked him about his feelings. He never got his LeapPad back, but she said too much screen time wasn't good for him anyway. He missed it for a long time. In the spring it got better. Or at least he was used to it.

And then somebody wanted to adopt him. Their names were Marnie and Phil, and they prayed all the time. They prayed for his soul every single day, and he had to wear pink dresses and answer to "Tammy." He started kindergarten, and he told his teacher he was really a boy and asked if could he be called Taz, please, and she called his parents. They did a lot more praying, and he had therapy all the time to talk about why he was sick and disturbed, and this went on until nearly spring again.

This time at least they told him in person. Marnie and Phil sat him down at the table. "You've been in our home nearly long enough to complete the adoption," Marnie said, "But this is not working. So, regretfully, we've told your social worker that she needs to find a different placement. We've decided to disrupt the adoption."

Taz swallowed.

"You can stay until she can find a placement," Phil said.

Marnie looked at him closely. "What are you thinking, Tammy?"

"I'm thinking I hate you," Taz said.

There were a bunch more families, three or four more placements. Taz lost count. He got a new social worker, an old lady named Ms. Valerie, who took him out to McDonald's and let him wear shorts and plain T-shirts. One time there was a couple there with a girl a little younger than he was. She had a tablet and asked him if he wanted to borrow it to play games while they got their food.

"No thanks," Taz said.

"Not again," he said to Ms. Valerie while they went off to the counter. "You're going to make me live with them whether I want to or not."

"You need permanency," Valerie said. "And that means being adopted. Taz, give them a chance. If you don't like them, there's no point. But I think you will. Jason and Jessica are very special people. And I think you'll like Allie too."

When they got their food and came over to the table with him and Valerie, they looked nervous. Taz looked at them seriously. "So, you want to adopt me. First of all, I'm unadoptable. Second of all, I'm a boy not a girl. Third of all, I have oppositional defiant disorder. So you can leave now and not waste our time."

Ms. Valerie sucked in a breath, but strangely Jessica started laughing. "Ok," she said. "That works for us."

In later years, Dad said that was the moment they'd decided to do it. "We knew you were our son right then," he said. "Brave, smart, and not a bit beaten down by everything you'd been through. We knew we belonged together."

"I didn't know it for a long time," Taz said. He was in high school and already taking hormones and he was competing in a track meet. Lots of parents would yell when their kids won, or just when they raced, but when Taz came pelting over the finish line in the relay, the last and strongest runner on the team, Jason had a big flashing LED sign that said "GO TAZ!" and a pair of antlers that hooted.

"WTF?" said Taz's teammate. "Who's that guy?"

Taz suddenly found himself completely choked up. "That's my dad," he said. "He's such a geek." And for a few minutes he couldn't talk at all because it was true.

———— • ————

Five years later he was in the middle of this military action. He was a medic, frontline stuff, not that anybody was ever really sure where the lines were.

They got the old guy stable and the doctor called for a helicopter. Taz checked the man's pulse again, thready but there.

"He's got a good chance if we can get an airlift," the doctor said. He sat back on his heels, two-day brown beard and a young face under the dust. "I'm Daniel. You?"

"Taz." He looked around, blood pooling on the floor under snuff cans and bags of chips. "This is crazy."

"Tell me about it," Daniel said.

"I don't know how we got here."

"I got here because I volunteered," Daniel said. "How about you?"

"Yeah." Taz shook his head. "It seemed like the right thing to do in '21."

"It still is," Daniel said. "But it's still crazy." He took a deep breath, then pulled his phone out of his pocket. The screen background was a beautiful Asian woman smiling. She held a little dog in her lap like it was waving to the camera. "That's my girlfriend, Amanda. I want to see if she texted." He glanced down at the screen for a minute. "Nothing new. She says be careful. Like I can do that."

The radio crackled. A helicopter was inbound, but they might be a few minutes because somebody had reported that MANPADs had been spotted in the area.

"That's not good," Daniel said. He put his phone down carefully and got up. "You watch this guy. I'm going to take a look."

Taz stayed down by the patient. "Are you sure that's a good idea?"

There was an explosion outside, a scream like someone in mortal pain. Daniel ran toward it.

———— • ————

"So he was killed," Taz said. "And I wasn't. Whoever it was with the MAN-PAD fired off a surface-to-surface missile." He was sitting at the countertop in his parents' apartment, a cup of coffee getting cold in front of him. Jason sat on the other barstool, his usually rumpled hair almost white. "Shit happens, right?"

"You can't forget what you've been through in a year," Dad said.

Taz shrugged. "It's just hard to believe it's over. I keep waiting for it to all happen again. That whole battle along the Colonial Pipeline..." He looked around the apartment. It was a lot smaller than the house they used to have, but Allie didn't live here anymore since she'd started working for an architectural firm drawing new buildings. And Dad and Mom were still telling their stories. Maybe people wanted stories more than ever. It was good to know that the stories were still there, right where they'd always been.

"It's over," his dad said. "And it's not going to happen again. The war is over." He looked down at his coffee. "And you did what needed to be done. You saved us all. You saved everything that mattered."

"Not everything."

"Ok, not everybody. But you can never save everybody."

"I know that," Taz said. Tears started in his eyes and he looked away. "I was the right person in the right place at the right time. And I did what I needed to do. That's all."

"That's being a hero."

Taz shrugged. "The ones who didn't make it, like Daniel—they're the heroes."

"I think that's always what young veterans say." Jason put his hand over Taz's. "So now what are you going to do? You could go back to school to be an RN or PA."

"I never want to do medicine again," Taz said.

"Then what?"

"Aquaculture." In that moment it suddenly seemed so clear, like the idea was born ready. "Sustainable fish farming. It's quiet. And we can always use fish, right?"

"Yeah," Jason said. "And you've got the rest of your life ahead of you."

Imbolc: The Storms of Winter

Taz, born in October 2000, occupies the same place on the wheel of the saeculum as Charles, born in 1923—the last cohort of the generation of young adults at the time of the crisis. Like Charles, his peers can expect to bear the brunt of the danger in the crisis. They are the generation of young heroes. Like Charles and his Greatest Generation, those who survive the crisis will move forward with extraordinary energy and purpose to rebuild the world afterward.

Responding to Taz's Story

- What is your immediate emotional response to Taz's story? Why do you feel that way?

- Do you identify with Taz? With others in his life? How are you similar? How are you different? If you share some of the same experiences but were shaped differently by them, why do you think that was?

- What do you think of Taz's experiences with foster care and adoption? Did you know that his experiences are not atypical? What does this say about the values of American society in the early twenty-first century?

- Did you notice Valerie as Taz's social worker? What do you think of Valerie at this point?

- What do you think of Taz's experience of growing up transgender in the 2000s and 2010s? How do you think his experience would be different if he were older or younger?

- What do you think of Taz's relationships with Jason, Jessica, and Allie?

- How do you think the difficult things in Taz's early life prepare him for his role in the crisis? What do you think will happen to him next?

- What do you think of Daniel's role in the crisis?

- What do you think of what has happened to Jason and Jessica since we last saw them in Allie's story? What do you think the rest of their lives will look like?

- What advice do you think Charles would give Taz if he could talk to him?

If you are also Autumn-born (1981–2001), consider these questions:

- Have you experienced some of the same social trends or experiences as Taz? How are those experiences the same or different?

- Do you know people who were in foster care? Who are transgender?

If you are not Autumn-born (1981–2001), consider these questions:

- If you are old enough to remember some of the trends and social movements of Taz's life, how did you experience them differently than he does? How was your understanding or perspective different?
- Does Taz remind you of people you have known, whether elders or juniors? How do you relate to those people? Do you know people who were in foster care? Who are transgender?
- How are Taz's experiences different from yours or those of people you know because of his moment in time?

The images of the crisis in Taz's story are imaginings, extrapolations of things that might happen. Within the context of the story, consider these questions:

- Why do you think Taz and Daniel are here? What are their motivations?
- What "side" do you think they're on? The United States? The Republic of California? The other United States? A militia? A transnational peacekeeping group?
- Where do you think the conflict is taking place? Is this part of a large zone of conflict, like the recent historical situations in the former Yugoslav republic or Syria, or is it a more isolated situation like the Boston Bombing or the Oklahoma City Bombing? Is this a war against another nation, a civil conflict, or a terrorist act?
- What do you think the resolution has been by the time Taz is talking to Jason? Who prevailed? What have the consequences been?

Allow yourself to imagine a number of different scenarios while trying to keep as neutral a viewpoint as possible. In other words, don't imagine either the best or worst possible situations. History rarely gives us either our grimmest imaginings or our most rosy-colored dreams. Real life usually lands somewhere in the middle.

And yet the hard thing is often to imagine at all—to see a future different from the fallacious eternal present. Toward that end, choose one particular issue or vulnerability you see in our nation at present and learn more about it. What are the issues that surround it? What are the reasons it may be a flashpoint? Try to choose a concrete and discreet example, not an overarching issue like racism or Russia. Pare it down to something smaller, like Russian bots on Twitter, where you can learn enough about it to be knowledgeable on the subject and understand how it works and might be a flashpoint.

Here is an example taken from the story above: the vulnerability of the Colonial Pipeline. It is a 5,500 mile long fuel oil pipeline from Houston, Texas, to New Jersey, carrying gasoline, home heating oil, diesel, jet fuel, and other fuels from the oil fields and refineries of Texas through the eastern seaboard and to the northeast. It is of critical strategic value, since without it the northeastern states would rapidly run drastically short of gasoline and other products, and it is uniquely vulnerable because of its great length, as it passes through eleven states and across many rural areas. A break, shutdown, or loss of control of the pipeline at any location would mean interruption of services for days, weeks, or longer. It also directly supplies "multiple Department of Defense installations each day."[36] Loss of operations would also impact the military as well as civilian use.

Now imagine some of the possible outcomes of the issue you have selected. For example, if the Colonial Pipeline were inoperable, what would the impact be on the northeast in winter for home heating fuel to become unavailable until it could be brought in by sea? What would the impact be in the I-95 corridor if gasoline were no longer available to distributors because of a pipeline shutdown? What would the impact be on, for example, North Georgia or Upstate South Carolina if control of the pipeline became a strategic target for military action?

Imagining the Possible

For this exercise you will once again need your notebook or preferred journaling method.

---

36. Colonial Pipeline website, http://www.colpipe.com/home/about-colonial/system-map, accessed March 23, 2019

You are creating a story like Taz's story about a future event. It doesn't have to come to pass, and in fact it probably won't. However, simply getting our heads around the idea that something—one of these things—will happen is vitally important. It helps us prepare ourselves for the parts of Winter still ahead. The difference between this story and Taz's is that you are the hero.

As we discussed earlier, media gives us examples of many different kinds of heroes. Which type do you identify with? Are you the healer, like Dr. Beverly Crusher or Dr. Carson Beckett? Are you the tech genius, like Tony Stark (Iron Man) or Samantha Carter? Are you a warrior, like Arthur Curry (Aquaman) or Diana Prince (Wonder Woman)? Are you a guide, like Obi-Wan Kenobi or Tia Dalma? Are you a ruler, like T'Challa (Black Panther) or Elizabeth Weir? Are you a trickster, like Natalia Romanova (Black Widow) or Lando Calrissian? Try to imagine what kind of hero you would be if you were in a hero story. And no, you probably won't be a superhero who saves the world twice before breakfast, but you can make a difference. You can be the hero. Someone will be, and it can be you.

Once you've decided which type of hero you are, then think about how that would play out in the scenario you've considered. A warrior might take direct action to protect people or to prevent something bad from happening. A guide might help others find their paths or be a spiritual counselor to those who have suffered trauma or lost loved ones. A ruler might maintain a physically safe space, make sure that essential services continue, and preserve the community. There are other roles, but these are some examples.

Now make up a story. When you were a child, you probably knew how to imagine yourself as a hero, but maybe it's been a long time since you exercised your imagination this way. Maybe you've gotten used to "being practical" or maybe you've internalized the idea that you can't be a hero—you're too old or not smart enough or not physically fit enough or some other reason. Maybe you've internalized that you're a failure. It doesn't matter why you may not have seen yourself as a hero because often the hero doesn't until "it happens." That's a narrative too—the hero is just this ordinary person who isn't special and doesn't have amazing powers, and then something happens that leads them to step up and put on the mantle of something greater than themselves, to grow into the role put before them. The events make the hero out of the supposedly ordinary person who was just living their life. That can be your origin story if you're having trouble seeing yourself as a hero.

Or maybe you're not. Maybe you've always secretly known you were special and were just waiting for an opportunity to show what you could do; that opportunity is upon you. Now is your moment.

What happens? What do you do? How do you respond and how do you take on the role of hero in this story?

Write or draw what happens. You can simply make notes or you can write a full story or draw these events. You can even write a song if you're so moved! Tell the story at least to yourself of how you responded heroically to the things that happened in the Crisis era. When you have told your story, keep it in your journal or somewhere else you can take it out and examine it when you need to.

Events may happen that test you. Know that you can rise to the occasion, as so many people have for so long. We are not weak, venal, selfish creatures no matter what some modern stories tell us. In real disasters, people help each other. In real crises, the good comes to the fore. In real trials, the selfish do not win. People succeed by working together, by cooperating and collaborating, and by helping each other. Nobody is strong enough to go it alone. A mix of skills, archetypes, ages, and experiences is the strongest model for a successful community. You are valuable and you are needed. Step up and be the hero that the season demands.

However, you need not do that alone. Now we will ask for help from deities appropriate to your service in a rite for two or more.

Asking for Divine Help

This rite is designed for a group of any size and as few as two people. However, it also can be done by one person. In all cases, review the entire ritual before performing it and adjust it according to your own circumstances, needs, and Pagan tradition.

Preparation

Prior to the ritual, each participant must have done the previous exercise and:

- Identified their strength or the type of hero they want to embody.
- Identified a deity that is appropriate to ask for help in becoming the role that they seek. This could be a god or goddess with whom they have a long relationship, the patron of a particular profession, a deity they're drawn to because of some appropriate attribute. The reason they choose that particular deity is entirely individual.
- Identified which cardinal direction is appropriate for their offering. The following chart will help people decide which altar they will be using.

East	South	West	North
communications: journalism, media, broadcast, information technology	first responders: firefighters, police, 911 dispatch	counselors and nurturers: psychologists, social workers, therapists	agriculture: landscaping, farming, beekeeping, horticulture
teaching and education: preschool to postgraduate	military and veterans	parents and caregivers, whether for the young, old, or those with disabilities	building and construction: masons, water and sewer, carpentry, roofing, etc.
medicine: doctors, nurses, PAs, dental hygienists, etc.	athletes of all types	social sciences: anthropology, religious studies, etc.	undertakers, medical examiners, hospice workers
physical scientists and mathematicians: chemistry, physics, etc.	advocates, lawyers and lobbyists, activists, political scientists	fishing, aquaculture, and those who work the sea in any way	judges and officers of the court
architects and designers	electrical trades, engineering	environmental sciences: biology, ecology, zoology, etc.	crafts and arts that work in clay, wood, stone, or other natural materials

Needless to say, this chart is not exhaustive, and there will be many gray areas that individuals will have to consider carefully, perhaps in conjunction with their concept of their relationship with the patron deity they plan to invoke. For example, one of my roles in the crisis is as a guardian ad litem, a court-appointed special guardian for children in foster care. If the patron goddess is Isis, it might seem that the best fit would be west, invoking Isis, the Mother of the World, and that would not be a bad choice at all. However, because my role is to be the eyes of the court, the handmaiden of justice, a better choice would be north, and to invoke Isis, the Lady of Amenti, she who sits in judgment over the living and the dead.

Another possibility would be to consider the focus of the work you do. For example, a nurse may work in many settings, from a clinical setting in a busy teaching hospital to being a public health nurse in a rural area or being a hospice nurse in a refuge for the dying. The first might see their role as falling in east, while the second might choose south for their work as an advocate for health among vulnerable populations, while the third might choose north for their role as a psychopomp. There isn't a right or wrong answer. Think carefully about how you want to fulfill your role.

It may also be that you have more than one role—for example as a caregiver and as someone who works in the building trades. In that case, choose which role best fits with the hero you have imagined yourself in the previous exercise.

What about artists and musicians? That's the complicated one, because it depends on the focus of their work. For example, a controlled, precise classical violinist might belong in east, while a folk-rock guitarist might belong in west. A goldsmith or a glasswright might belong in south, while a wildlife photographer might belong in north. Think about what the focus of your work is, both its purpose and the materials, subjects, and techniques you employ.

What about merchants, people whose primary job is to sell things? First of all, ask yourself if this is your vocation, the role you take as a hero, because many people who work in marketing or retail in this economy do so as a means to another end—to make money to live on while they pursue an art or craft, while they attend school, or to help them care for their family. If, however, your primary focus is a mercantile job, consider what it is you sell. For example, if you're a real estate agent whose goal is to help people find the right home, you may belong in north.

Once you have identified which direction you will choose, let's move on to the rite itself.

Supplies

five small tables that can serve as altars

five candles, either one each in white, yellow, red, blue, and green, or five
   white candles in colored or clear glass holders

incense and a suitable burner

a knife or sword that is used for ritual purposes

a pitcher of water and an empty chalice or cup

a dish of salt with a closable lid

a chalice of wine and a wide bowl

matches or a lighter

Optional extras:

altar cloths

images of deities your group prefers

seasonal flowers

a compass if you do not know which direction is north

Each participant should have:

ritual clothing according to their tradition

an offering to their deity. It may be as simple as a candle or incense, or it may
   be something you have made, either edible or not. (If you are doing this
   with a large group and you worry that someone will show up without,
   have a few extra votive candles on hand just in case!)

Setting Up

Ascertain which direction is north. Set four of your altars at the cardinal compass points, with the fifth altar in the middle of the circle that this makes.

Allow enough space for a person to walk around the outside of the circle—in other words, don't put the altars flush against the wall. There should also be enough space for someone to approach the central altar. How large a space you will need depends on the number of participants you intend to have, as everyone should be able to gather within the circle without having their hair, robes, or sleeves in the candles.

Set the yellow candle (and altar cloth if you are using one) on the eastward altar. Also put on this altar the incense (unlit) and incense burner. You will also want to put a lighter or matches nearby.

Set the red candle (and altar cloth if you are using one) on the southward altar. Also put on this the knife or sword, sheathed but not peace-bound.

Set the blue candle (and altar cloth if you are using one) on the westward altar. Also put the pitcher of water and the empty chalice here.

Set the green candle (and altar cloth if you are using one) on the northern altar. Also put the closed dish of salt here.

Set the white candle, images of deities, seasonal flowers if you are using them, altar cloth if you are using it, the chalice of wine, and the wide bowl on the central altar.

Arranging the Group

There are five speaking parts in this rite: four quarters and the officiant.

Each person with a quarter should stand at their appropriate altar while the officiant should stand in the middle. The rest of the participants, if there are more than five, should fill in evenly between the quarters—in other words, not everybody clumped on one side of the circle. Spread out so that approximately the same number of people are standing between each altar. Turn out any distracting electrical lights, electronic devices, phones, music, etc. Pause and take a deep breath.

The Rite

OFFICIANT: We gather as the ancients did, in the presence of the gods. We gather in peace and in harmony of purpose.

EASTERN QUARTER: *(Uses matches or lighter to light the yellow candle.)* Subsolanus, wind of the east, we call upon your blessing tonight. Rain-bearer, he who comes from the direction of the rising sun with sweet, life-giving moisture, we ask for your blessing. As you usher in the Spring with your gifts, we are grateful to you. *(Passes the matches or lighter to the southern quarter person.)*

SOUTHERN QUARTER: *(Use matches or lighter to light the red candle.)* Auster, wind of the south, we call upon your blessing tonight. Summer wind, who comes from the south with thunder and lightning, we ask for your blessing. As you lessen Summer's heat, we are grateful to you. *(Passes the matches or lighter to the western quarter person.)*

WESTERN QUARTER: *(Uses matches or lighter to light the blue candle.)* Favonius, wind of the west, we call upon your blessing tonight. Autumn wind who fills the sails of ships and shakes the apples from the tree, we ask for your blessing. As you send wild leaves flying, we are grateful to you. *(Passes the matches or lighter to the northern quarter person.)*

NORTHERN QUARTER: *(Uses matches or lighter to light the green candle.)* Aquilo, wind of the north, we call upon your blessing tonight. Winter wind who rules the icy gales and brings snow, we ask for your blessing. As you bring us clear, crisp nights, we are grateful to you. *(Passes the matches or lighter to the officiant.)*

OFFICIANT: *(Uses matches or lighter to light the white candle before the images if they are using them, or on its own if not.)* Jana, Jupiter, who reign above, be welcome to our gathering. We ask for your blessing this night. *[If you wish to substitute other names for the deities as your group prefers, you may. Jana and Jupiter are Roman names for the queen and king of heaven and are appropriate to this rite. If you wish to use deities from a different tradition, consider king and queen pairings.]*

EASTERN QUARTER: *(Uses the matches or lighter to light the incense and carefully steps behind the eastern altar. Elevates the burning incense, and then slowly walks clockwise around the outside of the circle, tracing the dimensions of the circle with the smoke. They are casting the circle in smoke, visualizing a safe and sacred space* *within. When they return to the eastern quarter, they place the burning incense on the altar.)*

SOUTHERN QUARTER: *(Unsheathes the sword or knife and carefully steps behind the southern altar. Using the blade, slowly walks clockwise around the outside of the circle, visualizing the tip making a line as they go, creating a safe and sacred space within. When they return to the southern quarter, they place the unsheathed blade on the altar.)*

WESTERN QUARTER: *(Pours some water from the pitcher into the chalice and carefully steps behind the western altar. Elevating the chalice, slowly walks clockwise around the outside of the circle, visualizing creating a safe and sacred space within. When they return to the western quarter, they place the chalice on the altar.)*

NORTHERN QUARTER: *(Opens the dish of salt and carefully steps behind the northern altar. Holding the dish, takes a small pinch of salt between their forefinger and thumb and scatters it as they walk clockwise around the circle. They may stop and get more salt from the dish as needed as they go, visualizing a safe and sacred space within the circle. When they return to the northern quarter, they place the open dish on the altar.)*

OFFICIANT: Jupiter and Jana, king and queen of heaven, we are grateful for your many gifts and for your witness to our intentions. *(Pours wine generously from the chalice into the offering bowl in libation.)* We have gathered here in your presence to ask for the assistance of the gods so that we can better serve here, in the world that is, in the world that we love and live in. We are of this earth. We are bound to this earth. This is our home. We are part of our communities, of our families, of our circles of love. As such, we take seriously our responsibilities to those communities, families, and circles of love. We share concern when those things are threatened, and we know that we must rise up as so many have before us and play our role in momentous events. We must be heroes. And yet we know that heroes need the help of the gods— tale after tale tells us how those who are inspired, who literally have the wind of life breathed into them by grace, do things that seemed impossible. We ask for that grace. We ask for that inspiration. Winds of the world, lords of heaven, breathe that inspiration into us that we may better serve!

EASTERN QUARTER: *(Steps forward with their individual offering and goes to the altar that they think is most appropriate to it. There, they state which deity they are addressing and what they ask of them. This part is highly individual and should be heartfelt and different for each person. They should state how they hope to serve and ask that deity's help. They should then leave the offering on the appropriate altar.)*

PERSON NEXT TO EASTERN QUARTER: *(Follows in turn. This could be the person on the southern quarter, or it could be someone in between. Each person should take their turn going clockwise around the circle. It may be that many people put offerings on the same altar and few put them on another, depending on the makeup of this group. That's ok. It may be that several people address the same deity. That's also ok. Each person should take as long as they wish.)*

OFFICIANT: *(Assists with logistics, including making sure that the matches or lighter are at hand if someone needs to light something and that there is room for things on the altars, etc. When everyone else has gone, the officiant goes last to make their offering. By now there may be quite a feeling of power building.)*

OFFICIANT: Please join hands. *(Everyone should join hands around the circle. The officiant can step into the circle at whatever place feels best. Allow a moment to let the energy flow and for everyone to bask in the glow of these intentions.)* We stand here unified by our purpose, knowing that as diverse as our talents, as different as our personal paths, we are not alone. We are together. We are brought together by our desire to work for the betterment of our community, for our families of choice, and by our love of the world. We are a superhero team. We are a band of heroes. We stand together, each contributing uniquely to the whole, joined by love. So may it be. *(Lets go of hands and turns back to the central altar.)* Jana and Jupiter, immortal queen and king, thank you for your gifts, your blessings, and most of all your love for us. Thank you for your presence here tonight and thank you to all those who have been called in witness and in devotion. *(Bows head for a moment.)* Thank you, great ones. *(Carefully extinguishes the white candle.)*

NORTHERN QUARTER: Aquilo, north wind, thank you for your blessing and your protection. *(Lifts the salt dish, steps carefully behind the northern altar, and proceeds counterclockwise around the circle, mentally sweeping up the line previously drawn to delineate the circle. When they have returned to the northern altar, they put the lid back on the salt dish and extinguish the green candle.)*

WESTERN QUARTER: Favonius, west wind, thank you for your blessing and your protection. *(Lifts the chalice, steps carefully behind the western altar, and proceeds counterclockwise around the circle, mentally removing the line previously drawn to delineate the circle. When they return to the western altar, they put the chalice down and extinguish the blue candle.)*

SOUTHERN QUARTER: Auster, south wind, thank you for your blessing and your protection. *(Lifts the sword or knife, steps carefully behind the southern altar, and proceeds counterclockwise around the circle, mentally removing the line previously drawn to delineate the circle. When they return to the southern altar, they sheath the blade and extinguish the red candle.)*

EASTERN QUARTER: Subsolanus, east wind, thank you for your blessing and your protection. *(Lifts the incense, steps carefully behind the eastern altar, and proceeds counterclockwise around the circle, mentally removing the line previously drawn to delineate the circle. When they returned to the eastern altar, they put out the incense and extinguish the yellow candle.)*

OFFICIANT: The circle is closed. May bright blessings follow us all.

Afterward

You may now break for cakes and ale, for other food, or whatever your group chooses to do. Food of some kind is recommended to help everyone ground.

It is recommended that at some point a designated person should take the water from the chalice and the wine in the libation bowl and empty them outside onto the ground as offerings. For the others, each person may then retrieve their offering to take home with them as a reminder of the rite and their commitments. If these are votive candles or incense, of course they should extinguish them before transporting them. If they are edibles, they may also be left outside with the water and wine at the donor's discretion, or they may be taken home for a home altar if they prefer.

You have made your plans for Winter. You are walking the path of the hero. Though cold winds may swirl around you, you have others at your side and the blessing of the gods to warm you.

Chapter 12

A New Beginning

After Winter comes Spring. Sometime in the mid-2020s the Crisis era will end. What do we imagine Spring to be and how do we see ourselves in Springtime?

Like the Crisis era itself, history teaches us that there are three phases of Spring corresponding to the three months of spring on the Wheel of the Year, the period from the Spring Equinox to Midsummer. Let's explore a little bit what the long-range forecast, based on historical modeling, can tell us to expect in the new saeculum. We are entering a new era, and this is the beginning of it.

Spring Equinox (Mid-2020s to Around 2030)

Spring has arrived, but the nights are still cold. There is frost on many mornings, and while crocuses and daffodils are opening in the growing sun, the days have a definite chill. It's possible there is one more storm left, though it will be mercifully brief. Each day the sun rises sooner, and the warmth of the sun promises the days ahead will be fine. We still have our heavy blankets, and we still know that our heating bills will be dreadful, but we can see that it won't be long before we put away the heavy sweaters and thick comforters in favor of our summer things. We celebrate with bunnies and eggs, with yellow and pastel things to lighten our homes, with hyacinths and golden daffodils.

The fruit trees light up with crowns of pink and white, blossoms that open in the bright morning. Spring is here!

On the Great Wheel, this is the very beginning of the new cycle. It is a time of incredible opportunity. The old order has been swept away, the fire of ekpyrosis has burned the old forest, and new seeds are sprouting. What will they be? What will the new order look like? What conflicts have been resolved and what conclusions have been reached?

Let's look at a historical model from the last Spring Equinox. In the cycle previous to that, the saeculum from 1866–1945, two domestic issues had dominated politics, first bursting into prominence in the Summer era before the turn of the century, and then becoming major political and social issues throughout the rest of the saeculum. Those two issues were temperance and suffrage.

The temperance movement advocated complete abstinence from all forms of alcohol and saw many social ills as arising from the consumption of alcoholic beverages. It sought to completely prohibit consumption of alcohol in the United States, a goal apparently achieved with the passage of the Eighteenth Amendment to the Constitution of the United States in 1919. This gave birth to the era of Prohibition, which lasted until the repeal of the Eighteenth Amendment in 1933. Temperance also created one of the most successful third parties in American history, the Prohibition Party, founded in 1869 and active until after World War II. With the new saeculum, it became irrelevant in the postwar world.

Suffrage, the idea that women should have the right to vote and run for elected office, first gained steam in the United States in the 1870s, and for a time the suffrage and temperance movements ran hand in hand. Many states passed laws allowing women to vote in local and state elections between 1880 and 1920, but women could still not vote in national elections. In 1920 the Nineteenth Amendment changed that and granted women the same voting rights as men. This has been the law since that time, and there have never been serious challenges to repeal it, or even mainstream rhetoric around repeal since World War II.

In other words, both movements became nationally important at the same time, both reached their apogee at the same time, and both reached complete resolution at the same time. Why were both essentially settled in the immediate postwar years, with one succeeding and one failing?

The answer lies in the Greatest Generation, the Autumn-born generation born between 1905–1925, who had just completely come of age in 1946. Having grown up with both temperance and suffrage, they all knew how they felt about both. As a generation, the Greatest Generation supported votes for women and opposed the prohibition of alcohol. Their opinion on these two issues settled them. This may seem like a simplification, but once they became the largest and most active voting bloc and continued to hold that position for the next fifty years, their position was unassailable. Imagine trying to repeal women's right to vote in 1960 or 1980! It was completely impossible. Now imagine trying to reinstate Prohibition in 1965 or 1985. Can you imagine any of the Greatest Generation presidents, from John F. Kennedy to George H. W. Bush, supporting either initiative? Can you imagine their voting peers supporting either? By the time the Greatest Generation exited the scene as national leaders, the questions had been settled for many decades. Changing the status quo had become unthinkable by the mid-1990s.

One important thing this tells us about the next new Spring is that some of the major issues of the last saeculum, some of the most divisive issues of the culture wars, will be definitively settled. The Millennials occupy the same position as the Greatest Generation, and their beliefs will be enshrined over the next half-century. It's possible to look at their opinions today and guess what some of those settled issues will be. For example, Millennials strongly support LGBT+ rights, more strongly than any other living generation. According to the Pew Research Center, the gold standard in social research, 74% of Millennials support gay marriage. (To note, 65% of Generation X does, 56% of Baby Boomers, and only 41% of Silents.)[37] For the Millennials, this major culture war issue is settled. As they become the dominant power in

---

37. "Changing Attitudes on Gay Marriage," Pew Research Center, June 26, 2017

American politics, conflicts over gay rights will seem as antique as the question of whether women should vote.

Another issue the Millennials seem to be reaching generational consensus on is gun control. According to a Quinnipac University poll on February 20, 2018, 68% of Millennials support stricter gun laws, 61% support a ban on the sale of assault rifles, 71% support a mandatory waiting period on gun purchases, and 99% support universal background checks.[38] It makes sense that the generation that has grown up with school shootings has firmly established opinions on the issue.

Therefore, it's reasonable to identify these as two culture war issues that are likely to be settled by 2030. Unless some event radically changes the opinions of millions of Millennials, their views will crystalize into law over the next five decades. Doubtless, there will be other issues settled that we cannot yet identify, generational majorities based on their experiences in the next few years. However, one thing we can be certain of is that the Millennials' consensus will create the status quo until the next Crisis era sometime around 2090, when their soon-to-be-elder children will fight a new culture war.

The period of the Spring Equinox is a period of promise. This is not to say that this is a time without conflict. However, most of those conflicts will be carryovers from the major conflict that just ended, not new fights about new issues. For example, in the last Spring one of the major sources of conflict in the 1946–1950 time frame was the question of borders in Europe. The United States, Britain, France, and the Soviet Union had established military zones of occupation that would eventually become spheres of influence, NATO and the Warsaw Pact. Conflicts like the Berlin Airlift and the seizure of Czechoslovakia were part of testing and amending these borders, in both cases an attempt by the Soviet Union to extend their power. One was successful. One was not. But these were not new issues. They were continuations of the ending of World War II.

If, hypothetically, the Crisis era ends around 2025 with the continental United States dividing into two or more new nations, there will be res-

---

38. Quinnipac University poll, Quinnipac University, February 20, 2018

olutions that will continue for the next years. Is a certain state part of one or the other? What if part of a border state wants to be in another entity? What if, for example, western Missouri wants to be with Kansas and Arkansas, but St. Louis and its environs want to be with Illinois? What about trade and treaties that have been disrupted? What about national assets, like satellites? We may continue to see low-grade conflicts, standoffs, and disputes that are essentially carryovers. If the United States remains one nation, there are likely to continue to be resolutions that must be reached, perhaps including a constitutional convention or other changes to the form of government. Remember, we are talking about a disruption on the scale of the American Revolution, the Civil War, and World War II. There will be major changes as a result. In the Spring Equinox era, those changes become established.

This is the amazing, once-in-a-saeculum opportunity! What the Millennials adopt will become reality for the next half century. What will that be? It depends on what they choose based on their experiences and their influencers. If you are a Millennial, you will choose. If you are not, you have the unique opportunity to influence what those decisions are through culture, art, politics, and your direct influence on those you know. Literally how you raise your children will shape the world. The stories you tell, the lessons you teach younger people with whom you come in contact, the cultural touchstones you exalt, will guide the hearts of the decision makers for decades. It is an awesome responsibility. Those influential touches are made now, and through the end of the crisis into the new dawn. After that, the Millennials' decisions will be enshrined as the new order coalesces.

Spring Full Blown (The 2030s)

The days are warm at last, and even the year's final frost barely touches the green and growing world. Now is the time for planting, for young animals, for gardens filled with sprouting seeds, new seedlings freshly transplanted, and every spring-flowering plant. Birds sing in the trees. Even rains bring beauty, for after them the world appears fresh-washed and born anew. In spring everything is growing.

So too in saecular Spring everything grows. Bigger, cleaner, brighter, and better—the dark Winter is over and everything can be accomplished! Now is the time to build, to take on ambitious projects. Immediately following the American Revolution, Spring came in the form of the young republic, their heady, fast days of growth when the United States took in more and more immigrants, when cities rose where towns had been, when Lewis and Clark explored the vastness of the continent. In the last Spring, in the 1950s, America transformed with interstate highways, gleaming office buildings, and plumbing and electricity came even to rural places.

In our next Spring, look for infrastructure growth. Technologies that are now nascent to harness wind and sun will become commonplace, an energy revolution that will extend to every part of life. Technologies like self-driving cars will also expand. Perhaps most trucking will become automated—why pay drivers who have to work limited shifts and take breaks when trucks can simply cross the country with no driver? The revolution in personal vehicles is already on the horizon—imagine the freedom for older adults if their car can take them shopping or to the doctor's office without them needing to drive, or the convenience of sending your car to pick up your groceries for you! One major pizza chain is already exploring this technology for pizza delivery.[39] In the 2030s it will be commonplace. Kids won't remember when pizza delivery involved a driver any more than Millennials remember the milkman!

Of course we cannot see exactly what all the changes will be, but we can look at technologies now in their infancy, as a person in 1939 could have guessed that air travel might become a major mode of transportation in the 1950s. We can also identify some of the problems that the new technologies will address, for example, dealing with hazards of climate change. Buildings designed to withstand wildfires or hurricanes already exist but are not in common use. These design principles could be adopted on a broad basis. This is not the distant future of science fiction, but fifteen to twenty years from now, as far in the future as the year 2000 is in the past.

---

39. Tim Higgins, "Pizza Delivery Gears Up for a Driverless Era," *The Wall Street Journal*, June 26, 2018

Spring is, comparatively, a very safe time. Social pathologies are reduced and death rates drop. To take one example of how this may play out, in 2016 more than 37,000 Americans were killed in motor vehicle crashes, the third largest cause of death in the US. Of these, 93%, or more than 33,400 people's deaths, were caused by driver error, either the driver who was killed or another driver. Imagine if self-driving cars were widely adopted. They cannot break traffic laws, won't speed, can't be drunk, won't weave in and out of traffic or drive recklessly. Imagine if 33,000 people a year didn't die. Imagine what it would mean to our society to suddenly remove the third most likely cause of death, or to greatly reduce its impact, say from 37,000 people a year to 7,000! That is simply one example of how the 2030s may be perceived as a safer decade and may in fact be much safer.

Unfortunately, safety may also come at the price of a loss of privacy. Already people are expressing concerns about the "internet of things" and the constant surveillance of our homes by the technology we purchase. How much compromise with privacy are we willing to make for safety and convenience? We do not yet know how this conflict will play out.

Another potential difficulty is the new "permanent record" created by our internet footprints. Do we really want everything we have ever done and said, every ill-considered retweet or rude joke, to be available to everyone forever? Perhaps the professional curation of personality will become a service for the job seeker and college applicant alike. Hiring a publicist may no longer be exclusively for celebrities, as everyone seeking a new job or opportunity faces the kind of scrutiny that has been reserved for the elite. Professional advice and curation may become commonplace in a world where we must watch every word we ever utter in fear that, in two years or twenty years, it will be deemed inappropriate. Job seekers and college applicants may also need professional stylists to create an appealing internet personality. It's already necessary for some prospective adoptive parents to have professional help to create the family "look" that will encourage birth mothers to place their children with them. As Russell Elkins of America Adopts says, "Your [birth parent book] is the most important marketing tool you have to connect with an expectant mother."[40] Will we need to market ourselves in every facet of our lives, with a sharp class divide between those who can afford professional curation and those who cannot?

And what about AI determining whether we qualify for mortgages or employment based on predictive profiles? What about the inherent biases written into these closed box programs? The *Wall Street Journal* reported that one major tech employer's AI routinely rejected resumés containing the word "women's" as in women's groups or women's colleges.[41] What laws are made around these new challenges are going to be central to how society develops in the new saeculum. It may be that cynical and suspicious Generation Xers will rein in Millennial data entrepreneurs in the name of privacy as they finally hold a plurality of elected offices in the 2030s.

Beltane (The 2040s)

Beltane arrives on the scene with warm nights and warmer days, the pale colors of early spring giving way to tropical hues, the world a green background for riots of color. The garden is growing, the baby birds are learning to fly, and clouds of pollen coat cars and porches. Summer is coming, just around the bend, though it's not here yet. Spring fever strikes. Wouldn't it be lovely to take the day off and lie in the grass?

A new generation is coming of age, children born after the Crisis era who don't share either the optimism or exhaustion of previous generations. Why is the world so safe? Why is the emphasis so completely on outward achievement rather than inward growth? Meanwhile, those who have been dissatisfied with the way the new order has coalesced have begun creating underground countercultures. These seeds will sprout as they are adopted by the rising generation who seek alternative ideas that feed their internal rebellions. For example, as elderly Lost Generation Pagan leaders like Gerald Gardner inspired Baby Boomer youth in the 1960s, so may elderly Genera-

---

40. "Tips for Creating a Realistic Adoption Profile and Birth Parent Book," adoptionmakesafamily.org, October 12, 2018

41. Sue Shellenbarger, "A Crucial Step for Avoiding AI Disasters," *The Wall Street Journal*, February 13, 2019

tion X leaders inspire the new Spring-born generation as we once again enter the season of Beltane in the 2040s.

Also, even as external achievements multiply, attention is drawn to problems that still remain or have newly developed. In the wake of the Civil War crisis, the rights of women began to come to the fore as they remained unaddressed. In the wake of World War II, civil rights for African Americans did the same. We do not yet know what the issues will be that rise in prominence. After the end of the Crisis era that may become clear, but as yet it's not possible to see what they will be. It is likely that some of them may rise from overreaching. While Autumn-born generations like the Greatest Generation and the Millennials have many strengths, their shadow is a tendency for hubris later in life. They've accomplished so much! Surely they know what's best. Surely they have the answers. In the 1960s this led Robert McNamara's "wonder kids" in the US Department of Defense to believe that fighting a war in Vietnam would be a cakewalk, and that victory could be accomplished quickly and easily by airpower.[42] They were wrong, and the Vietnam War turned out to be neither quick nor easy. We don't know how the Millennials may overreach, but it is certainly possible that they will.

However, we do know that at Beltane problems are addressed by law in a world that prizes justice and it seems that everything can be accomplished in time. There will be a sense that these problems are essentially solvable through cooperation, rather than the Summer belief that immediate and direct action is needed or the Autumn belief that these problems are essentially unsolvable. Instead, there is the sense that society can be improved through civil action because most people are essentially rational and fair, a complete turnaround from the beliefs of Winter. Late Spring is a time of hope.

Completing Your Wheel

As the Great Wheel continues to turn, you will turn with it through the seasons to come. The following chart is a map of the great year moving forward through the rest of the twenty-first century until today's youngest children

---

42. H.R. McMaster, *Dereliction of Duty: Lyndon Johnson, Robert McNamara, the Joint Chiefs of Staff, and the Lies that Led to Vietnam*, Harper Perennial, New York, NY, 1997

Date	Octave	National Mood	Elders	Maturity	Adulthood	Childhood
2020	Imbolc	grim	Silent and Baby Boom	Generation X	Millennials	Homelanders
2030	Spring Equinox	upbeat and conformist	Baby Boom and Generation X	Generation X and Millennials	Millennials and Homelanders	Homelanders and New Spring-born
2040	Beltane	fracturing and optimistic	Generation X and Millennials	Millennials	Homelanders and New Spring-born	New Spring-born
2050	Summer Solstice	frenetic and free	Generation X and Millennials	Homelanders	New Spring-born	New Spring-born and New Summer-born
2060	Lammas	complex and challenged	Millennials	Homelanders	New Spring-born	New Summer-born
2070	Autumn Equinox	divided	Millennials and Homelanders	Homelanders and New Spring-born	New Spring-born and New Summer-born	New Summer-born and New Autumn-born
2080	Samhain	darkening	Millennials and Homelanders	New Spring-born and New Summer-born	New Summer-born	New Autumn-born
2090	Winter Solstice	entering the crisis of 2100	Homelanders and New-Spring-born	New Spring-born and New Summer-born	New Summer-born and New Autumn-born	New Autumn-born and New Winter-born

occupy the niche of elders. Remember, all these dates are approximations. Events do not always happen exactly on the date, just as our changes of season depend on weather and where we live, and do not always occur precisely on the solstice or equinox. For example, in the last saeculum the Summer Solstice was clearly reached in 1969. Vietnam, the Summer of Love, the recent assassinations of Robert Kennedy and Martin Luther King Jr., Apollo 11 and the first moon landing, and massive cultural changes make 1969 the watershed moment. However, one would have predicted that the Summer Solstice would be in 1970. In actuality it was a year sooner. Events may shift these dates somewhat.

For this next exercise you will need your journal and your notes from chapter 3, when you went through the octaves going all the way around the Wheel of Life, remembering the parts you have already done and visualizing the parts yet to come. What you are going to do is combine the wheel of your own life that you already created with the Great Wheel turning forward.

We are now looking at the next saeculum, at the remainder of the twenty-first century. It may seem like these years and these events are impossibly far away, but they truly aren't. The youngest child you know will see them. That is what a saeculum is—the length of a long human life. When we next reach the Winter Solstice, the oldest Homelanders will be in their late eighties and the youngest in their early seventies. Like the child in the first story, the baby at the founding of the Etruscan village, some child you know will see in the twenty-second century and weather the crisis of 2100.

Your Wheel Turns

Let's take a look at how you will complete the circle of your life. You may wish to copy or draw the following chart to write in. If you are working your way through this book with a group or with others, there is a section especially for you after the initial exercise.

Look around the circle and find the location when you will be ninety years old. Hold that year in your mind.

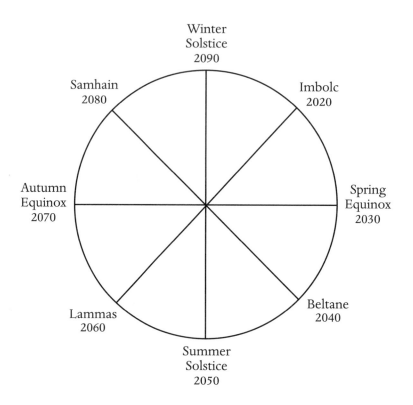

You are ninety. You are the elder, the wise old person who has lived a long and full life. You have reached comfortable old age, outlived many of your peers, and are now the dispenser of wisdom and wealth to a younger generation. You look back on your many years from the date that you have picked. Perhaps that's ten years in the future. Perhaps it's seventy. However long it has been, you have traversed the Great Wheel in its entirety, and are now back to the same season that you first experienced when you were ten years old. You have come all the way around and now stand on familiar ground having lived the cycle in full.

A young person, perhaps your grandchild or protégé, or perhaps a teenager doing an oral history project, wants to understand your experience. "What was it like to live then?" Visualize their face as they ask. "What was it like to live in 2020?"

Tell them. You can write your answers, draw them or otherwise illustrate them, or say them out loud as though you were explaining to them in person. Remember, this time is the past to the teenager. They know nothing about it except what they've read or seen. The past is a different country. You were once an inhabitant of this country, and they are asking you as someone who has come from a place they can only imagine but never visit.

- Where did you live? What did you value? What was 2020 like for you? What was the mood, the feeling of the time, the attitudes of people you knew?

- How is the present in which you are ninety years old different from 2020? Whether that present is 2030 or 2080, you are now in a familiar season, the one you first experienced when you were ten. What was the national mood when you were ten? What were the major social trends?

- Where was society on the spectrum from freedom to safety—were people mostly safe and craving freedom like 1970, or mostly free and craving safety, like 2010? Was it a transition period in between? Were leaders young and dynamic and optimistic, like 1960, or older and cynical like 2000? Were problems seen as public and global like 1940 or internal and personal like 1980? In the year that is your new present, when you are ninety, how do people approach life? What is the baseline mood? What are the conflicts about?

Now look at the external problems society faces in your new present:

- What problems that existed in 2020 have been solved? For example, is healthcare still an issue? How was the question resolved and when? What would a teenager in the new present be surprised about in regards to healthcare in 2020?

- What about climate change? Have we successfully reversed the warming trends? When did we do so, and what have been the impacts? When, if ever, will we return to climate stability? If this is 2040, perhaps we have ceased contributing to warming but the trend will continue for another twenty years before the effects abate. If this is 2080, perhaps this problem is history—something that people read about in books but no teenager has ever experienced. Or perhaps their new normal is something that would have been considered catastrophic in 2020. What do you tell them about it?

- How do people feel about Paganism as a minority religion? Is it accepted? Suspect? Derided as anti-scientific foolishness? Conflated with right-wing political views? Considered left-wing and anti-technology? Simply dismissed?

- Choose another issue that you care about—what has happened by the time you are ninety years old? What do people presume about it "today" in your new present? How is this different from 2020? Tell the teenager what it was like in 2020—and consider what the teenager's assumptions may be based on their own lifetimes.

Now the teen asks you the hard question. "What's going to happen to me in my life? If I live as long as you, what's going to happen next?"

Based on your accumulated wisdom, having lived through the entire cycle and having journeyed all the way around the Great Wheel, what is going to happen next? If you stand once again in the same season you stood in when you were ten years old, what will the next ten or twenty years of the teen's life encompass? For example, if you are now in 2035, deep in Springtime, moving toward the height of optimism and outward-looking power, you may foresee another Summer approaching. It may seem that the world is now safe and the pressure to conform to the new social norms is continually increasing, but you know that in the next twenty years that will fracture into the Summer of a new era. Alternately, if you now stand at the end of Summer, you know that Autumn will come, and that the majority of the teen's years will not be spent in the eternal Summer they have so far experienced, but in harder times of Autumn and Winter. What advice can you give them based on your life and times? What can you tell them about the saeculum, about the Great Wheel and how they too are living its cycle? Write, illustrate, or simply tell out loud what you would tell the teen.

If you are working through this book with a group, you may wish to role-play these scenes. Pair up and choose someone to play the teen and the other the elder. Play out the scenes creating a story—how do you relate to one another? Is this an oral history project or a grandparent and grandchild? Is your story the story of some particular population that you are passing on—for example, the story of an African American family like Charles, Valerie, Nikia, and Lucas? If you are taking roles in a story like that, what would Valerie say to Lucas? What would Nikia say to Lucas's child in due course of time, in 2068? What would another story in that family saga be, if for example you told the story of Charles's mother Ida, born in 1900 on a tenant farm and who moved into town to work in the hospital? Or of Rachel's father who fled Poland just before the Warsaw Ghetto closed down and escape became impossible? Or of Mike, Shirley's father, the fatherless child of an Irish woman born in Brooklyn before the turn of the century? The history of the US is the history of us. What is the piece of the story that you are telling?

If you are working through this book and are part of a larger group, for example an outer temple or a Unitarian Universalist congregation, here is a way to present your work to the larger group. Those who wish to perform should select roles as elders or teens and choose a date in the future that is the new present. Role-playing these scenes, the teens can lead the elders to talk about the experiences of their lives, while the elders will explain the concepts of the great year and its ever-turning wheel.

We dance the mystery, all together.

Liminal Time

Now it's time to pull together all we have learned. Around 2020 we are still standing at Imbolc on the Great Wheel. On our Wheel of Life, the octave between Imbolc and the Spring Equinox is liminal time, the transition from one life to another. We have said farewell to our old body and our old identity, to our old ties and our old life. We are dead. We have passed out of one life and have not yet begun another. We are undergoing our own personal ekpyrosis, an environment lying fallow and empty as a scorched land that was once a forest waits under cover of snow for the melt and sun that will bring forth fields of wildflowers. Soon we will once again feel the need to be and inhabit a body. Soon we will be born, somewhere on this vast planet, to some people. We will step out of liminal time and onto the wheel again.

So too does this octave represent liminal time on the Great Wheel, the dark Winter that society experiences when we are in the throes of ekpyrosis. We are ending one cycle but we have not quite yet begun another.

In Roman religion, the god who presided over such liminal moments was Janus. We know him because he gives his name to January, the first month of the year, and he was very important to the Romans. He was the god of beginnings and endings, of thresholds and doorways, those places where one is neither inside nor outside. Often pictured in classical art as a bearded man with two faces, one looks toward the past and one toward the future. His holy days were the first day of each month, especially the hour of the night when the day changes, the moment that is the last of one month and the first of the next. This day, called the *kalends* of a month, was when he received libations. Janus was also often symbolized by a key, that which opens a door, gate, or portal and allows passage from one state to another. He was also celebrated on January 1, when he received official sacrifices as he presided over the turning of the year.[43]

Ancient poets such as Ovid and Macrobius presented him as also ruling over liminal moments in human lives, such as the passage between childhood and adulthood. Festus and Livy also describe a rite of Janus that was essentially a demobilization rite, a ritual through which soldiers returning home after the end of a war were cleansed of the blood they had shed, ritually removed their warrior's accoutrements, and then, veiled, passed beneath a beam that was a symbolic portal to the city and to civilian life. On the other side they would lift the veil, a new man who had returned home.[44] As a god who ruled over borders, Janus also stood apart from typical Roman family life. Macrobius tells the story that he loved a mortal king named Camese and

---

43. Ovid, *Fasti*

44. Georges Dumezil, *Archaic Roman Religion*, translated by Philip Knapp, Johns Hopkins University Press, Baltimore, 1996

shared his rule of Latium until Camese's death, after which Janus dwelled alone.[45]

Because of Janus's association with the turning Wheel of the Year and his attribute of looking both backward and forward in time, he is the ideal god for us to ask to bring everything that we have learned about the Great Wheel together into a rite. Remember, as we stand in Winter we cannot go back. We cannot return the world to the way it was ten years ago or twenty or forty. The only way out of our present season is to turn the wheel forward into the next season, to the inevitable Spring that follows Winter. In February it is not possible to tape last season's leaves back on the trees! However, it is possible for spring to come early, or for winter's storms to abate in the weeks after Imbolc. A mild winter, an early spring—these are things to pray for and to work for—but returning to autumn is impossible. Therefore, our rite will ask Janus to turn the wheel forward.

Invoking Janus, God of Liminal Time

This rite is best performed on the first day of the month. Ideally, this would also be New Year's Day, January 1, but any first of the month is a suitable time for a rite invoking Janus. This rite is written for nine voices, an officiant and one person who will represent each octave of the Wheel of the Year; however, you may certainly double up people as necessary for a smaller group. It is also suitable for a large group, or it can be adapted for one person. In all cases, read the entire rite before performing it and adjust it according to your needs and tradition.

Preparations

Before the ritual, ask each participant to think about what happened in these various years: 1960, 1970, 1980, 1990, 2000, and 2010. The events may be big, important public events, events in popular culture, or events in their own lives like a marriage, the birth of a child, their first job. They should have this in mind coming into ritual.

---

45. Macrobius, *Saturnalia*

Octave	Altar Cloth Color	Candle Color	Additional Dressings	Really Creative Additional Dressings
Beltane	bright pink or floral print	bright pink	flowers in a vase, especially roses and lilies	a pillbox hat, a pair of vintage shoes with kitten heels, a vinyl record from 1960, mid-century toys
Summer Solstice	orange or bright boho print	orange	a potted green plant	macramé anything, a pair of fringed boots, a vintage camo jacket, a vinyl record around 1970, a tambourine
Lammas	purple or paisley	purple	a basket containing summer vegetables	toy cars, an 8-track or cassette tape, memorabilia from a movie around 1980, a vintage T-shirt
Autumn Equinox	dark blue or a star print on a dark background	dark blue	a vase of autumn flowers	a VHS tape, studded leather bracelets, a hair bow, a Baby on Board sign, a concert T-shirt from 1990
Samhain	black or black and metallic	black	a pumpkin, real or artificial	a music CD, a flannel shirt, toys for X-Men or The Fellowship of the Ring or another movie around 2000, a Harry Potter book

Octave	Altar Cloth Color	Candle Color	Additional Dressings	Really Creative Additional Dressings
Winter Solstice	dark green	dark green	holiday greenery, whether real or artificial, holly, ivy	an iPod, *Dora the Explorer* toys, yoga pants, Crocs, comic book movie memorabilia
Imbolc	white	white	a white bowl containing an egg	smartphone (silenced), athleisurewear, slime, *Fortnite* and *Game of Thrones* memorabilia
Spring Equinox	pale yellow, pale green or lavender	yellow	spring flowers, either real or artificial	nothing

Supplies

eight small tables to serve as altars

one large table to serve as a central altar

eight colored candles (see chart on pages 186–187) and one white candle

incense and a suitable burner (myrrh or laurel is appropriate, or sandalwood
if you prefer)

a knife or sword used for ritual purposes

a pitcher filled with water and a chalice

a box of salt with a lid

a chalice of wine (with an additional carafe to refill it if you have a large
group)

a libation bowl

a lighter or matches

a bowl of dates with enough dates for everyone present to have one (dates
are a traditional offering to Janus and a traditional food for his celebrations)

Optional extras:

a plate of cakes, cookies, or crackers made with spelt flour, preferably savory
rather than sweet (savory spelt cakes were a Roman offering to Janus,
especially ones crusted with salt, like a salt bagel)

an image of Janus and/or a symbol of Janus, such as a key

dressings for the eight side altars (see chart on pages 186–187)

music and a way to play it (ideas for a playlist follow)

What you are doing is creating a circle that will mirror the Great Wheel
from 1960 to 2030, mapping the Great Wheel to the familiar form of the
Wheel of the Year. The really creative altar dressings are to help you link the
altar not just to the season but to the year that it correlates to on the Great
Wheel. For example, the Winter Solstice altar not only contains the seasonal
greenery and dark green candles one might expect, but items that we might
associate with the year 2010, things that were popular or significant. All of
the items in the really creative altar dressings column are ideas to get you
started—you can choose anything that evokes the year for you, and a group

of people can have fun planning out what those items might be. However, if that seems like too much work, bear in mind that the altar dressings are completely optional. You can simply use the candles and nothing else if you prefer.

If you are using an image of Janus, a key, or the plates of spelt cakes, place them on the central altar with the white candle and dates. Also place the wine chalice and libation bowl there. If you have an additional carafe, you can either place it on the altar if it is attractive, or beneath it if you have room below and prefer to keep it out of the way.

You may also wish to have a playlist of music that will set the stage for your rite, particularly if you are doing it with a large group and you know that people are going to be milling around before the rite and afterward gathering for refreshments. If so, you can easily find lists of the hit songs for each year from 1960 to 2020. (Obviously we do not yet know what the top songs from 2030 will be!)

Setting Up

Each person who is speaking for an octave should stand at their appropriate altar while the officiant should stand in the middle. Four of the people speaking for an octave will also participate in the quarter calling, those on the Spring Equinox, Summer Solstice, Autumn Equinox, and Winter Solstice. The rest of the participants should fill in evenly between the octaves—in other words, not everybody clumped on one side of the circle. Spread out so that approximately the same number of people are standing between each altar. Turn off any distracting electrical lights, electronic devices, phones, etc. Pause and take a deep breath.

The Rite

OFFICIANT: We gather as the ancients did, in the presence of the gods. We gather in peace and in harmony of purpose.

SPRING EQUINOX: *(Uses matches or lighter to light the yellow candle.)* Subsolanus, wind of the east, we call upon your blessing tonight. Rain-bearer, he who comes from the direction of the rising sun with sweet, life-giving moisture, we ask for your blessing. As you usher in the Spring with your gifts, we are grateful to you. *(Pass the matches or lighter to the southern quarter person.)*

SUMMER SOLSTICE: *(Uses matches or lighter to light the orange candle.)* Auster, wind of the south, we call upon your blessing tonight. Summer wind, who comes from the south with thunder and lightning, we ask for your blessing. As you lessen Summer's heat, we are grateful to you. *(Pass the matches or lighter to the western quarter person.)*

AUTUMN EQUINOX: *(Uses matches or lighter to light the blue candle.)* Favonius, wind of the west, we call upon your blessing tonight. Autumn wind who fills the sails of ships and shakes the apples from the tree, we ask for your blessing. As you send wild leaves flying, we are grateful to you. *(Pass the matches or lighter to the northern quarter person.)*

WINTER SOLSTICE: *(Uses matches or lighter to light the green candle.)* Aquilo, wind of the north, we call upon your blessing tonight. Winter wind who rules the icy gales and brings snow, we ask for your blessing. As you bring us clear, crisp nights, we are grateful to you. *(Pass the matches or lighter to the officiant.)*

OFFICIANT: *(Lights the white candle on the central altar.)* Janus, god of doorways and of keys, of beginnings and of endings, two-faced god who sees the future and the past, we call upon you to attend to us. We are in need of your wisdom and we humbly ask for your presence and blessing. *(Pours wine into the libation bowl as a libation.)*

SPRING EQUINOX: *(Uses the matches or lighter to light the incense and carefully steps behind the eastern altar. Elevates the burning incense, and then slowly walks clockwise around the outside of the circle, tracing the dimensions of the circle with the smoke. They are casting the circle in smoke, visualizing a safe and sacred space within. When they return to where they began, they then pivot to the center and place the burning incense on the central altar rather than the side altar.)*

SUMMER SOLSTICE: *(Unsheathes the sword or knife and carefully steps behind the southern altar. Using the blade, slowly walks clockwise around the outside of the circle, visualizing the tip making a line as they go, creating a safe and sacred space within. When they return to where they began, they then pivot to the center and place the unsheathed blade on the central altar rather than the side altar.)*

AUTUMN EQUINOX: *(Pours some water from the pitcher into the chalice and carefully steps behind the western altar. Elevating the chalice, slowly walks clockwise around the outside of the circle, visualizing creating a safe and sacred space within. When they return to where they began, they then pivot to the center and place the chalice on the central altar rather than the side altar.)*

WINTER SOLSTICE: *(Opens the dish of salt and carefully steps behind the northern altar. Holding the dish, takes a small pinch of salt between their forefinger and thumb and scatters it as they walk clockwise around the circle. They may stop and get more salt from the dish as needed as they go, visualizing a safe and sacred space within the circle. When they return to where they began, they then pivot to the center and place the salt dish on the central altar rather than the side altar.)*

OFFICIANT: Janus, we stand in your liminal time. We are between. We stand in Winter, and yet we know that Spring will come. We ask you, who looks backward and forward both, to turn the wheel. We begin.

BELTANE: *(Lights the pink candle.)* I am the season of Beltane, fire in the blood and fire on the hill. 1960. John F. Kennedy is elected president. Woolworth's sit-ins spark desegregation of lunch counters. The first American soldiers are sent to Vietnam. Sputnik is the first satellite to orbit the Earth. What else happened in 1960? *(The officiant may need to begin or urge participants to call out appropriate things. They may be historic events or personal events, e.g., "I started high school!" When people have had a chance to participate, the officiant nods to the Summer Solstice person.)*

SUMMER SOLSTICE: I am the season of Summer Solstice, hot days and hot nights. 1970. The first Earth Day. Apollo 13 suffers catastrophic failure but the astronauts return to Earth safely. Four students are killed by National Guardsmen at Kent State. Doonesbury begins publishing. What else happened in 1970? *(Again, people may need to be invited to call out events, whether historic or personal. "I was born!")*

LAMMAS: *(Lights the purple candle.)* I am the season of Lammas, the first harvest, the season of sacrifice. 1980. US hostages in Iran are finally released. Ronald Reagan is elected president. Mount Saint Helens erupts. Everyone wants to know "Who shot J. R.?" What else happened in 1980? *(By now people should be getting the hang of contributing, but the officiant may still need to prompt.)*

AUTUMN EQUINOX: I am the season of Autumn Equinox, the season of harvest, the first chill in the air. 1990. The World Wide Web is founded. The Cold War ends. The Gulf War begins. The Hubble Space Telescope is launched. What else happened in 1990? *(Again, people may call out their contributions.)*

SAMHAIN: *(Lights the black candle.)* I am the season of Samhain, the season of the final harvest, the end of the growing season. The year 2000. The PlayStation 2 is released. George W. Bush is elected president in a hotly contested election. The International Space Station gets its first crew. The Y2K bug turns out to be nothing. What else happened in 2000? *(Again, people may call out their contributions. This is probably becoming spontaneous and natural.)*

WINTER SOLSTICE: I am the season of Winter Solstice, the season of gathering together against the cold. 2010. Nine states recognize same-sex marriage. 2010 is the warmest year ever recorded to date. Obamacare becomes law. The last US combat troops leave Iraq. What else happened in 2010? *(People know what to do now and can call out contributions.)*

IMBOLC: *(Lights white candle and waits for everyone to get quiet, and then another moment for everyone to become just a little uncomfortable.)* I am the season of darkness before dawn, of bitter cold, of endings and beginnings. 2020. What happens in 2020? What will happen in this octave before us?

OFFICIANT: *(Quietly.)* We do not know.

IMBOLC: We do not know. We stand in the blowing snow and we look for the path. It is beneath the snow. We can't see it. We do not know the way forward. We do not know how to get home.

BELTANE: *(Quietly.)* Trust in love.

IMBOLC: Will love be our guide? We do not know the path.

SUMMER SOLSTICE: Trust in strength.

IMBOLC: Will strength be our guide? We do not know the path.

LAMMAS: Trust in friendship.

IMBOLC: Will friendship be our guide? We do not know the path.

AUTUMN EQUINOX: Trust in family.

IMBOLC: Will family be our guide? We do not know the path.

SAMHAIN: Trust in wisdom.

IMBOLC: Will wisdom be our guide? We do not know the path.

WINTER SOLSTICE: Trust in the gods.

IMBOLC: Will the gods be our guide? We do not know the path.

OFFICIANT: Janus, god of beginnings and endings, you who rule over liminal time, over these moments when the world ends and then begins, show us the path!

SPRING EQUINOX: I am waiting.

OFFICIANT: Did you hear something?

SPRING EQUINOX: I am waiting. I am here beyond the moment in which you now dwell. I am here.

OFFICIANT: Janus, can you guide us forward into the new Spring?

SPRING EQUINOX: Turn the wheel.

ALL TOGETHER: Turn the wheel. *(Officiant encourages everyone to join in.)* Turn the wheel. Turn the wheel. Turn the wheel!

SPRING EQUINOX: I am the season of Spring Equinox, the bright morning of new beginnings, of hope and the world reborn. 2030. Who knows what promise I hold for you? Who knows what gifts I have for you in the new Spring?

OFFICIANT: Now we will walk this wheel together. The wheel turns. Please join hands outside the ring of the altars. *(When everyone has joined hands, slowly begins to circle the wheel clockwise, so that each person is passing each altar in the correct order, going around the outside of the circle along the lines previously traced. This may get faster as it goes. When everyone has gone around three times and returned to their starting location, the officiant stops the turning.)* Janus, we have turned the wheel forward!

SPRING EQUINOX: Welcome to Springtime.

OFFICIANT: *(Lifts the chalice.)* This is the gift of the harvest, of the year that was. *(Goes around the circle clockwise, offering each person a sip. If you need additional wine, that is what the carafe is for.)* This is the gift of the year to come, sweetness that awaits you. *(Goes around the circle clockwise, offering each person a date from the plate of dates. If you have a plate of spelt cakes or crackers, the officiant takes them up now.)* This is the work of our hands, grain and salt, water and fire. *(Goes around the circle clockwise, offering each person the chance to break off a piece.)*

ALL THE OCTAVES: The wheel turns.

OFFICIANT: We thank you. Janus, he who looks forward and backward at once, thank you for your wisdom as we walk the Great Wheel. *(Extinguishes the white candle.)*

WINTER SOLSTICE: Aquilo, north wind, thank you for your blessing and your protection. *(Retrieves the salt dish, steps carefully behind the Winter Solstice altar, and proceeds counterclockwise around the circle, mentally sweeping up the line previously drawn to delineate the circle. When they have returned to the Winter Solstice altar, they put the lid back on the salt dish and extinguish the green candle.)*

AUTUMN EQUINOX: Favonius, west wind, thank you for your blessing and your protection. *(Retrieves the water chalice, steps carefully behind the Autumn Equinox altar, and proceeds counterclockwise around the circle, mentally removing the line previously drawn to delineate the circle. When they have returned to the Autumn Equinox altar, they put the chalice down and extinguish the blue candle.)*

Summer Solstice: Auster, south wind, thank you for your blessing and your protection. *(Retrieves the sword or knife, steps carefully behind the Summer Solstice altar, and proceeds counterclockwise around the circle, mentally removing the line previously drawn to delineate the circle. When they have returned to the Summer Solstice altar, they sheath the blade and extinguish the orange candle.)*

Spring Equinox: Subsolanus, east wind, thank you for your blessing and your protection. *(Retrieves the incense, steps carefully behind the Spring Equinox altar, and proceeds counterclockwise around the circle, mentally removing the line previously drawn to delineate the circle. When they have returned to the Spring Equinox altar, they put out the incense and extinguish the yellow candle.)*

Officiant: The circle is closed. May bright blessings follow us all.

Afterward

You may break now for cakes and ale, for other refreshments, or whatever your tradition prefers. You may wish to resume playing your playlist if you have one. You may allow the altars to remain set up for a while so that everyone can walk around and observe everything on them. Remember to take outdoors the wine in the libation bowl and any other food offerings and allow them to return to the earth.

You have walked the Great Wheel all together. May you do so in life as you have in ritual.

····· Chapter 13 ·····

The Wheel Turns, Spring-Born: (2025?–2045?)

Sometime in the mid-2020s, a baby will be born who is the first of a new generation. They will be the oldest of the children who don't remember the Crisis era, to whom "what happened then" is just a story. It's a thing old people talk about, a big show they missed, the most important thing ever as far as the old people are concerned, but of little importance to them. They are focused on the future.

And what a future it will be! Technologies that were in their infancy in 2020 will change the world—whether those are solar technologies, reusable rocket boosters, or embedded microchips. Problems that seemed unsolvable are taken in stride, falling to their parents' teamwork and civic spirit. In this generous world, why are old people so concerned about risk?

The parents of the first cohorts of this generation are for the most part Millennials, though as the decades pass into the 2030s more and more of them are Homelanders. Raised to be safe at all costs, their parents have created a cozy world for many of them. Everything is planned, clean, and orderly. Interventions target any deviation with many good results and some bad. When is a line crossed between healthy and unhealthy thoughts? What is the boundary between individual and abnormal?

As the first Homelanders reach thirty-nine, the season of Lammas, somewhere in the early 2040s, they will begin to wonder about their own lives and choices. They will attempt to refine the world the Millennials have built, to make it more nuanced, merciful, and beautiful. Perhaps there are shades of gray. Perhaps there are multiple right answers and the idea that you pick the correct one out of four choices was false all along. They will begin to push back against Millennial certainty and against Millennial entrepreneurs who have built the new behemoths in industry and technology, reining in these entities through regulation and antitrust law.

Meanwhile, the new Spring-born generation will have never perceived these entities as scrappy start-ups but as technocrats who possess outsized power, much as the Baby Boomers derided the "military-industrial complex." We cannot yet see, at Imbolc, what issues will explode into importance at Midsummer, or what the attitudes will be of a generation yet unborn, but we can know that it will happen. The Great Wheel will turn and the Spring-born will seek new answers that are in opposition to their parents' dominant culture, whatever form that takes. The heroes of the crisis of 2020 will be astounded, just as Charles was by Valerie's rebellion. However, aging Generation X won't be surprised at all. Here we are again, as my father said.

Lia's Story: Beltane

When Lia arrived on campus at her state's flagship university in August 2043, her entire family came to help her get settled—her mom; her stepdad, Jack; and her two younger brothers, who were eleven and eight. Lia was a lot older than they were and Jack was her stepdad because her real dad had died in the war before she was born. Of course she didn't remember him at all. Her mom had married Jack when she was five, and he was a good dad, though sometimes Lia wondered what her real father would have been like. Her grandmothers had his phone and she had heard his voice on it and on the videos he'd recorded for her mom when she was pregnant. A medic had brought them the phone after the war. His voice made him seem close, like he might walk in anytime.

"He was a doctor," her mother said. "And so smart. That's where you get it—being good at science and being clever and empathic. Daniel would be so proud of you. He died so you and other kids like you would have a good life."

Lia knew she had a lot to live up to. Everyone said so. Brighter, clearer, bigger, better—she was six when the wind turbine farm went up near them, eight when the power completely switched over. When she visited her grandmothers, Rachel and Linda, there were enormous concrete breakwaters to keep back the sea along the harbor, monumental white walls of curved concrete that looked like giant seashells. It was still getting warmer every year and would for a while because carbon emissions had been cut too late, so the sea was rising. She was eleven when Greenland lived up to its name, and she did a report in school on the satellite picture of formerly glaciated hills covered in green summer grass. When she was thirteen, she had to shelter in place at school while a wildfire burned through, but the school had been built to stand it, so everyone was safe. Afterward she took a selfie next to the melted soccer goal.

But these were challenges that could be met, and every day bright new buildings were rising that could stand the seas or storms, bright engineers paving the way to a completely interconnected world, and beyond. At night she could stand outside and watch the Argo being assembled in high Earth orbit, the sun glinting off its massive solar panels, the ship that in two years was going to take a colony to Mars.

When Lia started college with a major in biochemistry, Mars was her goal. They weren't going to build just one station. It took a lot of the best and brightest to populate a planet.

And yet sometime in her sophomore year, things began to chafe. It was too far to go home for spring break, so she went to her grandmothers' instead. Rachel and Linda were always glad to see her in the ranch house they'd shared since her father was a little boy, with its ramps for Linda's wheelchair. It wasn't just because she was eighty-seven. She'd used a wheelchair as long as Lia could remember.

"I broke my back during the war." She always told the story the same way. "There was a Militia attack on the airport and we were warned to evacuate the control tower. But we had a Qantas 767 coming in on great circle route on the end of its fuel, and I stayed to pass it off to control from another field. There were 268 people on board. They had to have a safe place to land. But it took too long. I waited too late." Linda shrugged.

"Why?" Lia had asked. "If they told you to evacuate…" Everyone was always supposed to evacuate when they were told to. It was a rule.

"I was the senior controller. I sent everyone else down and did it myself." She shrugged again. "I don't regret it."

Linda was Lia's favorite grandmother, with her cropped white hair and her no-nonsense way. She didn't make things sound better than they were, which was why Lia sat up with her that night during spring break after Rachel went to bed, sitting by her desk in the cramped study with its computer equipment and gaming stuff. "Why don't you get a smart wall?" Lia asked. "Instead of this keyboard thing?"

"I don't want a smart wall," Linda said. "Those things work two ways. I won't have surveillance cameras in this house."

"Everybody does," Lia said carefully.

"Not everybody."

"Well, not everybody who's old." Lia made it a joke. And then she frowned, trying to figure out how to put it so it didn't sound crazy. "Some people take cameras out. Some people take their chips out."

"That's true," Linda said. "You have the legal right to have your chip out after you're eighteen. It's there so your parents can always track you with GPS, but you're an adult now, so if you want it out, you can get it out."

"Only criminals do that," Lia said, but she squirmed because she knew it wasn't true. "And people who have something to hide."

"Everybody has things to hide," Linda said. "Everybody needs privacy." She picked up her cup of tea. "There's always tension between safety and freedom. Go too far either way and people get hurt. If you ask me, we've gone too far."

Lia swallowed. "Can you keep a secret?"

"Absolutely."

"Some people I know at school, they know some people in town. And one of them has a friend that has a place called 'the Land.'" She looked to see if Linda was reacting, but she wasn't. "It's a house up in the hills a long way from anything. It has solar panels so there's power, but it's out in the middle of nowhere, with no neighbors for miles. And there is no cable, no dish, no hot spot, nothing. They don't have any cameras or smart walls or anything and you're not even allowed to bring your phone when you come. You have to leave it in your dorm. And just go. Nobody knows where you are and nobody can reach you. You just go. There's like, no safety net at all."

"Did you go?"

"Not yet."

Linda smiled. "That's honest. Have fun."

"What?"

"Go. Have fun."

"But anything could happen." Lia gulped. "Anything at all. And nobody would ever know exactly what happened. There wouldn't be any footage or audio or messages or anything! There could be tobacco or sex or …" She ran out of possibilities.

"Sure could." Linda looked positively cheerful. "Just like when I was growing up. When I was your age being a lesbian was illegal. Now being queer is all about two innocent boys who love each other very much. It used to be transgressive, dangerous, sharp as a knife, and sweet as honey." She smiled, and for a second she looked just like that young sailor in her white uniform in the framed picture in the living room. "It's a dance, my darling Lia. It's fire and wind and drums on the mountain. Go jump off a cliff."

"I can't," Lia murmured. "What will my mother say?"

"Nothing, if you don't tell her." Linda smiled again. "I won't."

———— • ————

On the first weekend in May, Lia left her phone by her bed in her dorm and got into a vehicle with her friend Caden and her friend Isla and some guy named Grayson that they knew and once they were past the city and turned off the interstate they had to switch from control-drive mode to just self-driving because control didn't go this far out. They wound up the hills, passing fewer and fewer lights. It must have been two hours before they stopped at a gate. Grayson got out and opened it manually. It wasn't even electronic, and he didn't have a phone with him to swipe, so he opened the gate and they drove through the board and wire fence like something out of a movie and closed it behind them. Grayson jumped back in. "We're on the Land now," he said.

Light leaped ahead, a firepit on a hill in front of a big old house that curled into the trees. There were ten or twelve people already there, all around her age, laughing and talking. One girl had a fiddle, which was absolutely natural because what could be more folk than acoustic fiddle? There was beer and music and yes, somebody had tobacco cigarettes and talked about how they were part of real American culture, but Lia didn't try them because they made Isla nauseous when she did. It got late and after a while it was just her and Caden sitting out on a blanket by the dying fire and the stars overhead were more and brighter than she'd ever seen.

"It's getting cold," Caden said. "You want my jacket?"

"Sure," Lia said, and let him put it around her. His arm stayed around her, and that was even better. Nobody knew where she was. Nobody was documenting this, another milestone for her permanent record.

"It's weird, isn't it?" Caden said. "To think that we're completely off the grid. Completely on our own." Lots of times they were thinking the same thing at the same time.

"I like it," Lia said. "We could do anything or be anybody, and nobody would ever know. Nobody will ever know for sure what we say to each other or what we do. It's just us, like people in the Stone Age. Just us here, under the stars. Radical privacy activists."

Caden glanced up. "There might be satellites."

Lia saw the cliff in front of her, felt it like wind in her feathers, the heady feeling like a young hawk poised on the edge, waiting for the updraft. It was amazing. "We could go inside," she said. "There are no satellites there." And she kissed him.

When he came up for air, Caden said breathlessly, "We could."

And so they did, going into the house with their arms around each other's waists. Behind them, the fire burned out.

Above, the stars turned on in their dance, the wheel turning and turning again.

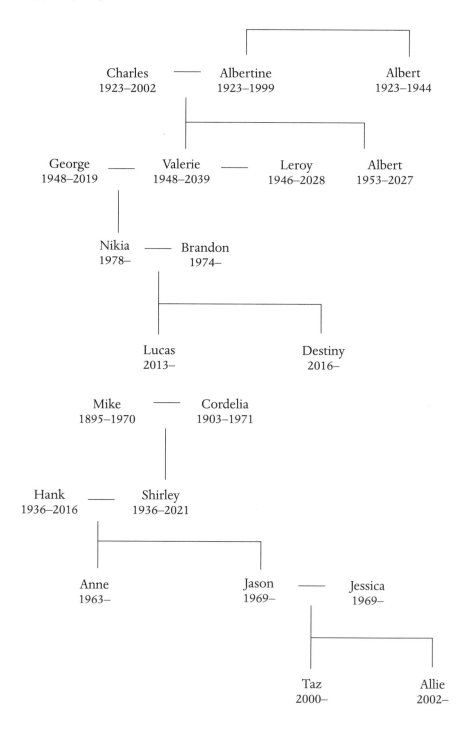

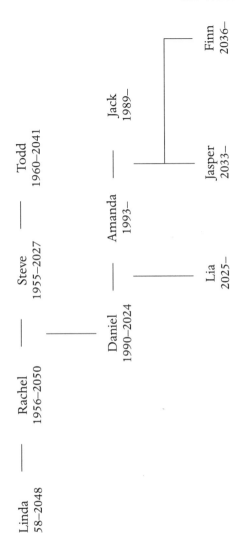

Bibliography

adoptionmakesafamily.org. 2018. *Tips for Creating a Realistic Adoption Profile and Birth Parent Book.* October 12.

Arrington, Debbie. 2016. "Wildfires, Wildflowers Are Part of California's Cycle of Life." *The Sacramento Bee.* July 29.

Benet, James. 1964. "Growing Up Pains at UC," *San Francisco Chronicle.* November 15.

Bowden, Mark. 1997. "Black Hawk Down," *The Philadelphia Enquirer.* November 16.

CBS News. 2011. "Average US Life Expectancy Tops 78." June 8. Accessed January 5, 2019.

Class120.com. 2018. *Parents.* Accessed April 6, 2019.

Colonial Pipeline. n.d. *About the Colonial Pipeline.* Accessed March 23, 2019.

de Grummond, Nancy Thomson. 2006. *Etruscan Myth, Sacred History, and Legend.* Philadelphia: University of Pennsylvania.

Dumezil, Georges, and Philip translator Knapp. 1996. *Archaic Roman Religion.* Baltimore, MD: Johns Hopkins University Press.

Eisley, Loren. 1969. "The Star Thrower." In *An Unexpected Universe.* New York: Harcourt Brace.

Elmore, Tim. 2014. "Homelanders: the next generation." *Psychology Today.* February 22.

Friedan, Betty. 1963. *The Feminine Mystique*. New York: W.W. Norton & Company.

Fukuyama, Francis. 1992. *The End of History*. New York: Simon & Schuster.

Higgins, Tim. 2018. "Pizza Delivery Gears Up for a Driverless Era." *The Wall Street Journal*, June 26.

Howe, Neil, and William Strauss. 1993. *13th Gen: Abort, Retry, Ignore, Fail?* New York: Vintage Press.

Laes, Christian, and Johan Strubbe. 2014. *Youth in the Roman Empire*. Cambridge, UK: Cambridge University Press.

Leeds, Jeff. 1992. "Child Poverty Grew in the 1980s." *Los Angeles Times*, August 12.

Livingston, Gretchen. 2014. "The Demographics of Remarriage." *Pew Research Center*, November.

Macrobius. n.d. *Saturnalia*.

McCarthy, Niall. 2018. "When Will the US Lose the Last of its World War II Veterans?" *Forbes*, May 28.

McMaster, H.R. 1997. *Dereliction of Duty: Lyndon Johnson, Robert McNamara, the Joint Chiefs of Staff, and the Lies that Led to Vietnam*. New York: Harper Perennial.

1983. *The Day After*. Directed by Nicholas Meyer.

Olin, Randi. 2015. "Why I won't be GPS tracking my college freshman." *The Washington Post*. October 29.

Ovid. n.d. *Fasti*.

Peters, Jeremy W. 2017. "Bannon's Views Can Be Traced to a Book That Warns, 'Winter Is Coming.'" *The New York Times*, April 8.

Pew Research Center. 2017. *Changing Attitudes on Gay Marriage*. June 26.

Quinnipac University. 2017. *Quinnipac University Poll*, February 28.

Reif, Jennifer. 1999. *The Mysteries of Demeter*. York Beach, ME: Samuel Weiser and Associates.

Rosenmeyer, Thomas. 1989. *Senecan Drama and Stoic Cosmology*. San Francisco: University of California Press.

Sass, Sorem A., and E.J. Gottfried. 1996. *Polio's Legacy.* Washington, DC: University Press of America.

Shellenbarger, Sue. 2019. "A Crucial Step for Avoiding AI Disasters." *The Wall Street Journal,* February 13.

Strauss, William, and Neil Howe. 1991. *Generations: The History of America's Future.* New York: Morrow and Company.

———. 1992. "The New Generation Gap." *The Atlantic Monthly,* December.

———. 1997. *The Fourth Turning.* New York: Broadway Books.

Turfa, Jean Macintosh. 2007. "The Etruscan Brontoscopic Calendar and Modern Archaeological Discoveries." *Etruscan Studies, Volume 10, Article 13.*

US Department of Defense. 2018. *Statistics About the War in Afghanistan.* Accessed December 4, 2018.

US Department of Health and Human Services. 2017. *Number of Children in Foster Care Continues to Increase.* November 30. Accessed May 19, 2018.

———. 1991. *Trends in Foster Care.* October 8. Accessed May 19, 2018.

To Write to the Author

If you wish to contact the author or would like more information about this book, please write to the author in care of Llewellyn Worldwide Ltd. and we will forward your request. Both the author and publisher appreciate hearing from you and learning of your enjoyment of this book and how it has helped you. Llewellyn Worldwide Ltd. cannot guarantee that every letter written to the author can be answered, but all will be forwarded. Please write to:

Jo Graham
℅ Llewellyn Worldwide
2143 Wooddale Drive
Woodbury, MN 55125-2989

Please enclose a self-addressed stamped envelope for reply,
or $1.00 to cover costs. If outside the U.S.A., enclose
an international postal reply coupon.

Many of Llewellyn's authors have websites with additional
information and resources. For more information,
please visit our website at http://www.llewellyn.com

GET MORE AT LLEWELLYN.COM

Visit us online to browse hundreds of our books and decks, plus sign up to receive our e-newsletters and exclusive online offers.

- Free tarot readings • Spell-a-Day • Moon phases
- Recipes, spells, and tips • Blogs • Encyclopedia
- Author interviews, articles, and upcoming events

GET SOCIAL WITH LLEWELLYN

Find us on  🐦 @LlewellynBooks

www.Facebook.com/LlewellynBooks

GET BOOKS AT LLEWELLYN

LLEWELLYN ORDERING INFORMATION

 Order online: Visit our website at www.llewellyn.com to select your books and place an order on our secure server.

 Order by phone:
- Call toll free within the US at 1-877-NEW-WRLD (1-877-639-9753)
- We accept VISA, MasterCard, American Express, and Discover.

 Order by mail:
Send the full price of your order (MN residents add 6.875% sales tax) in US funds plus postage and handling to: Llewellyn Worldwide, 2143 Wooddale Drive, Woodbury, MN 55125-2989

POSTAGE AND HANDLING

STANDARD (US): (Please allow 12 business days)
$30.00 and under, add $6.00.
$30.01 and over, FREE SHIPPING.

CANADA:
We cannot ship to Canada. Please shop your local bookstore or Amazon Canada.

INTERNATIONAL:
Customers pay the actual shipping cost to the final destination, which includes tracking information.

Visit us online for more shipping options.
Prices subject to change.

FREE CATALOG!

To order, call
1-877-
NEW-WRLD
ext. 8236
or visit our
website